unicef

United Nations Children's Fund

TIME FOR RIGHTS

Activities for Citizenship & PSHE for 9 – 13 year olds

Save the Children

Contents

The question

The child stands facing the teacher
(This happens every day);
A small, embarrassed creature
Who can't think what to say.

He gazes up at the ceiling,
He stares down at the floor,
With a hot and flustered feeling
And a question he can't ignore.

*Education should develop the
child's abilities to
their fullest potential.
(Article 29)*

*All organisations should work
towards what is best for the
child. (Article 3)*

He stands there like the stump of a tree
With a forest of arms around.
'It's easy, Sir!' 'Ask me!' 'Ask me!'
The answer it seems, is found.

*Children have a right to be
listened to, and to receive
appropriate information.
(Articles 12 & 13)*

*Discipline should not damage
the child's sense of dignity.
(Article 28)*

The child sits down with a lump in his throat
(This happens everywhere),
And brushes his eyes with the sleeve of his coat
And huddles in his chair.

*'Heard it in the playground'
by Allan Ahlberg.
Published by Viking 1989*

The UN Convention on the Rights of the Child

This publication celebrates the progress made in children's rights since **the UN Convention on the Rights of the Child** was adopted by the United Nations General Assembly on 20 November 1989. The Convention's development was a result of unprecedented co-operation amongst governments and non-governmental organisations from around the world.

The Convention in education

However, in the UK, it has taken over 10 years for teaching about the Convention to enter curricula, and even then it is not always specifically named. Why are adults so fearful of children knowing that they, too, have rights and are citizens, while constantly bemoaning young people's lack of responsibility? Wherever it has been taught, adults have been pleasantly surprised that, far from reinforcing alienation between the age groups, it has in fact improved behaviour and respect for others, of all ages.

Human rights acts

Meeting children's rights is also meeting their basic needs so that every child in the world can develop to their full potential. The Universal Declaration of Human Rights, ratified in 1946, automatically included children, but children have special needs which they cannot meet themselves. Children need protection and nurturing if they are to become fully functioning adults – hence the UN Convention on the Rights of the Child, which specifically focuses on how the special needs and rights of children should be met.

The UN Convention on the Rights of the Child spells out standards that governments are obligated to keep.
It was created with four basic principles in mind:
1.   The right to non-discrimination (Article 2).
2.   The right to have the child's best interest considered in all actions concerning children (Article 3).
3.   A child's right to life, survival and development (Article 6).
4.   A child's right to be heard (Article 12).

This last principle has proven the most contentious. It recognises children as citizens who are entitled to have their own views, and to have opportunities to express these views on issues that concern them. Understanding that they will be listened to is essential if children are to grow up understanding how to participate fully in society.

The Human Rights Act, which entered English law in October 2000, reinforces both the Universal Declaration and the Convention by making legal provision for people to challenge infringements of their rights, and this includes children.

The UN Convention on the Rights of the Child contains 54 Articles in three parts

Part 1: Articles 1 to 41 lay out specific rights for all children in terms of provision and protection. These can be divided into articles that describe the rights children have for survival, development, protection and participation in society.

Part 2: Articles 42 to 45 describe how the Convention should be brought into practice and monitored by a Committee on the Rights of the Child.

Part 3: Articles 46 to 54 outline the process by which the Convention comes into force through ratification by governments, or "State Parties" as they are termed.

The Convention in the United Kingdom

The United Kingdom government ratified the Convention on 16 December 1991. It has subsequently made two reports on the rights of children in the United Kingdom to the United Nations Committee on the Rights of the Child.

By signing the Convention in 1991, the UK promised to take action to ensure that the rights it contains are respected and enforced for all children in this country. However, the UK has placed reservations on two articles: The UK, excluding Scotland, reserves the right to place children in prisons together with adults in breach of the Convention; and, with regard to immigrant/refugee children, the UK reserves the right to implement national legislation over and above, or contrary to, the requirements of the Convention.

The Convention worldwide

By 1991 every country in the world (except Somalia and the United States of America) had ratified the Convention, making it the most universal statement on rights achieved during the twentieth century.

The Convention on the Rights of the Child encourages governments to act always in the best interests of children and to do all they can to implement the rights contained in the Convention. The responsibility includes promoting national awareness of the Convention and the provision of overseas aid.

Summary of the UN Convention on the Rights of the Child

In the Convention, the word 'child' means anyone under the age of 18.

Article 1
Everyone under 18 years of age has all the rights in this Convention.

Article 2
The Convention applies to everyone, whatever their race, religion, abilities, whatever they think or say, whatever type of family they come from.

Article 3
All organisations concerned with children should work towards what is best for each child.

Article 4
Governments should make these rights available to children.

Article 5
Governments should respect the rights and responsibilities of families to direct and guide their children so that, as they grow, they learn to use their rights properly.

Article 6
All children have the right to life. Governments should ensure that children survive and develop healthily.

Article 7
All children have the right to a legally registered name, the right to a nationality and the right to know and, as far as possible, to be cared for by their parents.

Article 8
Governments should respect children's right to a name, a nationality and family ties.

Article 9
Children should not be separated from their parents unless it is for their own good, for example if a parent is mistreating or neglecting a child. Children whose parents have separated have the right to stay in contact with both parents, unless this might hurt the child.

Article 10
Families who live in different countries should be allowed to move between those countries so that parents and children can stay in contact or get back together as a family.

Article 11
Governments should take steps to stop children being taken out of their own country illegally.

Article 12
Children have the right to say what they think should happen when adults are making decisions that affect them, and to have their opinions taken into account.

Article 13
Children have the right to get and to share information, as long as the information is not damaging to them or to others.

Article 14
Children have the right to think and believe what they want and to practise their religion, as long as they are not stopping other people from enjoying their rights. Parents should guide their children on these matters.

Article 15
Children have the right to meet together and to join groups and organisations, as long as this does not stop other people from enjoying their rights.

Article 16
Children have a right to privacy. The law should protect them from attacks against their way of life, their good name, their families and their homes.

Article 17
Children have the right to reliable information from the mass media. Television, radio and newspapers should provide information that children can understand, and should not promote materials that could harm children.

Article 18
Both parents share responsibility for bringing up their children, and should always consider what is best for each child. Governments should help parents by providing services to support them, especially if both parents work.

Article 19
Governments should ensure that children are properly cared for, and protect them from violence, abuse and neglect by their parents or anyone else who looks after them.

Article 20
Children who cannot be looked after by their own family must be looked after properly, by people who respect their religion, culture and language.

Article 21
When children are adopted, the first concern must be what is best for them. The same rules should apply whether the children are adopted in the country where they were born or taken to live in another country.

Article 22
Children who come into a country as refugees should have the same rights as children born in that country.

Article 23
Children who have any kind of disability should have special care and support so that they can lead full and independent lives.

Article 24
Children have the right to good quality health care and to clean water, nutritious food and a clean environment so that they will stay healthy. Rich countries should help poorer countries achieve this.

Article 25
Children who are looked after by their local authority rather than their parents should have their situation reviewed regularly.

Article 26
The Government should provide extra money for the children of families in need.

Article 27
Children have a right to a standard of living that is good enough to meet their physical and mental needs. The Government should help families who cannot afford to provide this.

Article 28
Children have a right to an education. Discipline in schools should respect children's human dignity. Primary education should be free. Wealthy countries should help poorer countries achieve this.

Article 29
Education should develop each child's personality and talents to the full. It should encourage children to respect their parents, and their own and other cultures.

Article 30
Children have a right to learn and use the language and customs of their families, whether these are shared by the majority of people in the country or not.

Article 31
All children have a right to relax and play, and to join in a wide range of activities.

Article 32
The Government should protect children from work that is dangerous or that might harm their health or their education.

Article 33
The Government should provide ways of protecting children from dangerous drugs.

Article 34
The Government should protect children from sexual abuse.

Article 35
The Government should make sure that children are not abducted or sold.

Article 36
Children should be protected from any activities that could harm their development.

Article 37
Children who break the law should not be treated cruelly. They should not be put in prison with adults and should be able to keep in contact with their families.

Article 38
Governments should not allow children under 15 to join the army. Children in war zones should receive special protection.

Article 39
Children who have been neglected or abused should receive special help to restore their self-respect.

Article 40
Children who are accused of breaking the law should receive legal help. Prison sentences for children should only be used for the most serious offences.

Article 41
If the laws of a particular country protect children better than the articles of the Convention, then those laws should stay.

Article 42
The Government should make the Convention known to all parents and children.

A Universal Declaration of Human Responsibilities

Children's rights are a special case because many of the rights laid down in the Convention on the Rights of the Child have to be provided by adults or the state.

However, the Convention does also refer to the responsibilities of children, in particular to respect the rights of others, especially their parents (Article 29).

Here are some suggestions of the responsibilities that could accompany rights.

- If every child, regardless of their sex, ethnic origin, social status, language, age, nationality or religion, has these rights then they also have a responsibility to respect each other in a humane way.

- If children have a right to be protected from conflict, cruelty, exploitation and neglect, then they also have a responsibility not to bully or harm each other.

- If children have a right to a clean environment, then they also have a responsibility to do what they can to look after their environment.

- If children have a right to be educated, then they have the obligation to learn as much as their capabilities allow and, where possible, to share their knowledge and experience with others.

- If all children have a right to a full life, then they should also lend help to the needy, the disadvantaged and the victims of discrimination so they can also enjoy this right.

- If children have a right to freedom of thought, conscience and religion, children also have the obligation to respect other's thoughts or religious principles.

Derived from a Universal Declaration of Human Responsibilities, by an organisation called World Goodwill, composed of ex-heads of state.

A history of children's rights

Eglantyne Jebb, an Englishwoman, first thought that there should be a children's charter after she and her sister helped homeless, starving children in Europe after the First World War. In 1919 they founded **The Save the Children Fund** in London.

In 1924, Eglantyne created a statement of children's rights called **The Declaration of Geneva**, which was adopted by the League of Nations (the forerunner of the United Nations). However, the Declaration and the League of Nations were rendered useless and powerless by outbreak of the Second World War in 1939.

The United Nations was founded in 1946, after the Second World War. **UNICEF, the United Nations International Children's Emergency Fund,** was created at the first meeting of the UN General Assembly in 1946. The work of **UNICEF** was similar to that of **Save the Children**, to help children in Europe after the war.

In 1948, the UN General Assembly adopted the **Universal Declaration of Human Rights**, which automatically includes children.

In 1959, on 20 November, the UN General Assembly adopted the **second Declaration of the Rights of the Child**. A declaration is not legally binding and does not carry an implementation procedure.

In the 1950s and 60s, Save the Children and UNICEF, now known as the United Nations Children's Fund, continued to work for children in Africa, Asia and Latin America.

1979 was the United Nations International Year of the Child. A working group was set up to draft a convention of children's rights, which would specifically meet the needs of children and have more status than the Declaration of Children's Rights. All member countries of the United Nations could take part.

On 20 November 1989, the United Nations General Assembly adopted* the UN Convention on the Rights of the Child.

By 1996 every country in the world (except Somalia and the USA) had ratified* the **UN Convention on the Rights of the Child**. It is the only human rights document that has been signed by almost all countries, making it the most universal statement of rights.

'Adopted' and 'ratified' are the technical terms used to indicate the 'legal' status of the Convention.

Questions and answers about the UN Convention on the Rights of the Child

This section seeks to provide answers for some commonly asked questions about the Convention.

Q. What are rights?

A. All people have rights, both legal and civil. They are the political, social and other advantages to which a person (including a child) has a just claim, morally or legally. They are laid down in a number of ways:

- Laws introduced by Parliament, e.g. the right to education, to free healthcare, to child benefit, etc. The Human Rights Act of October 2000 will help enforce the rights in the Convention.

- Rights developed at an international level, e. g. the United Nations Convention on the Rights of the Child and the Universal Declaration of Human Rights, then agreed to by individual governments.

Q. What does the Convention say about children's rights?

A. It recognises that children:

- Are young and vulnerable, and need special rights to protect them from harm.

- Need to be provided with education.

- Need to be provided with the best possible healthcare, family life and an adequate standard of living.

- Should learn to respect their parents.

- Although under 18 years old they are also citizens and have participation rights, i.e. to hold opinions and have them listened to, although, as in all consultative processes, there is no obligation to act on those opinions.

Q. Who has agreed that children should have these rights?

A. The Convention on the Rights of the Child was written by all member states of the UN and was adopted* by the United Nations on 20 November 1989, now celebrated as International Children's Rights Day.

Q. Has the United Kingdom agreed these rights?

A. Yes, the government ratified* the Convention on 16 December 1991.

Q. Have all countries ratified the Convention?

A. All but two countries have ratified. The ones which have not ratified the Convention are Somalia and the United States of America.

Q. Why should children learn about their rights in school?

A. It is the duty of each country that ratifies the Convention to see that children and adults learn about these rights (Article 42).

- New curricula recognise that children need to be taught about human and legal rights and responsibilities. The Convention on the Rights of the Child is about meeting the needs of children and is, therefore, the most appropriate human rights act for them to learn about at primary school.

Q. What does a child's right to participate mean?

A. The Convention recognises that children are citizens too, and it says that children are entitled to have their own views, and to have opportunities to express these views on issues that concern them.

- Every day parents and carers make many decisions on behalf of children. Parents have a duty to listen, consider and take children's opinions seriously in matters that concern the child.

- Participating in discussions about events that concern them helps a child to take responsibility for themselves and their views.

- It encourages them to express an opinion but also to realise that their opinion is not the only one to be considered.

- It gives them the opportunity to learn how to exercise their rights and take responsibility, within a safe environment.

Q. Will learning about rights affect children's behaviour?

A. Yes. Children learn through the experience of having their rights respected. In learning about rights, children also learn about the responsibilities that are involved in all people having equal rights.

- Those schools, and parents, which respect children's right to be consulted, and who treat children with respect, have found this reciprocated. Children also behave better towards each other.

Q. Isn't how families raise their children their own affair?

A. The Convention states that government shall make every effort to keep families intact, and provide support and assistance to parents in fulfilling their primary responsibilities with regard to the upbringing and development of their children.

- All parents rely on government policies regarding benefits, health and social services and provision of education opportunities to support the raising of their children. The Convention reinforces governments' obligations towards children and their families.

Q. What can children do, if after learning about their rights, they realise that they are being denied one or more?

A. Children, or adults acting on their behalf, should take up the matter with the relevant authority, e.g. the school, local council, with their MP, or seek legal advice.

Q. Do children in other countries learn about these rights?

A. Yes. In many countries of the world children both learn about and practise these rights in their schools.

Teaching Citizenship

I SAID TODAY WE WOULD LEARN
ABOUT DEMOCRACY.
I DID NOT ASK FOR YOUR
OPINION!

-NICK

Time for Rights in the curriculum

All four jurisidictions of the UK are giving increasing emphasis to allowing time in the curriculum for personal, social and health education and aspects of good citizenship. The majority of schools already include some, if not all, of the topics, knowledge, attitude and skill development now appearing in the different curricula.

Time for Rights attempts to provide a useful handbook for teachers to use in association with these curriculum areas. It provides active learning opportunities for developing a wide range of knowledge, attitudes and skills, which can be matched to several subject areas. The activities are applicable to a range of ability levels so it is usable by teachers of upper primary, lower secondary and middle school pupils.

As will be expected from a resource from the two leading children's rights organisations, our emphasis is on how the rights laid down in the UN Convention on the Rights of the Child can be integrated into the curriculum. Some of the activities are not new, but the relevance to children's rights may be.

The units in this resource contain activities that help prepare our children to participate as citizens through:

- Building **self-esteem, self-confidence and a sense of identity**;
- Emphasising **respect** for one's self and others, including **developing a healthy, safe lifestyle**;
- Developing **respect for cultural difference** and **diversity**;
- Teaching that **rights bring responsibilities** and that **the rights and welfare of others and oneself are defended and promoted**;
- Building awareness of **democracy and democratic procedures**;
- Developing **communication** and **co-operation skills**, including suggestions for building a cooperative classroom;
- Developing **oral skills** for **discussion, debate** and **presentations**;
- Suggesting ideas for **assemblies, forums, research**, etc.;
- Showing **global interdependence**, often through case studies of the lives of children in other parts of the world;
- Building community links by suggesting **homework tasks** which involve parents and carers.

Children as citizens

If children are to be empowered as citizens then they need to learn in an environment that recognises them as citizens; treats and respects them as citizens, and provides opportunities to practise and then develop skills which make people responsible citizens. Therefore the environment needs to reinforce learning through experience.

The aspect of the UN Convention on the Rights of the Child that possibly has had most impact, because to some it is so radical, is the child's right to give an opinion and be listened to - Article 12. **Time for Rights** provides many opportunities for this through carefully structured activities which encourage children to form and voice opinions while also listening to and respecting others. Without opportunities for practise, and to make mistakes in a safe environment, how can children develop the skills and attitudes that will encourage and enable them to play a responsible, active role in the community, country and beyond?

This publication can be used in many ways but we do recommend that Unit 1 **What are children's rights?** is done in some depth; activities in the following Units can then be undertaken with an informed perspective.

Children cannot recognise their rights and responsibilities in just one hour; there will be diverse and conflicting attitudes and behaviour to work through. But, if reports from schools which have undertaken this are anything to go by, we can guarantee that the rewards at the end are worth the commitment of time.

Active learning methodology

This resource uses methodology that develops skills of oral self expression, thinking, listening and speaking with respect. The key skills of listening and expression are developed through children being encouraged to speak, being listened to and then receiving a thoughtful, considered response.

Despite the emphasis on oral work in PSHE and Citizenship curricula, and also the importance placed on articulacy by employers, developing speaking skills does not receive the time and attention it deserves in the curriculum. More often it is pushed out by the pressure of meeting attainment targets, usually through written tasks which can be more easily measured. To develop oral skills pupils need to talk for a purpose, which means also being listened and responded to, which means valuable class time. Hence our emphasis on structured pair and group work where discussion can take place and all take part, and pupils can become their own critical listeners.

Here are our practical suggestions for introducing positive and productive lessons

A. List and discuss

'List and discuss' is a way of collecting ideas and thoughts in an organised way for a time-pressured environment. Some organisation is done while suggestions are made, they can then be discussed once all suggestions are listed.

Step 1
Ground rules – to be agreed and displayed:
- Children give their immediate thoughts on a topic or question;
- There are no 'right or 'wrong' answers;
- No answer is censured or commented upon;
- All suggestions are written down;
- Answers are a word or phrase.

Step 2
- Present the topic to be discussed and write it on the board. If information is to be collected which will be compared and contrasted, make this clear and show how it is to be organised, usually in columns.
- The period when pupils give their thoughts should be limited to a few minutes. You will probably want them to put their hands up to contribute.
- List their contributions – if you organise the information as you go, ask the contributor in which column the information should be placed.
- When time is up for contributions, look at the result and discuss. This may involve re-organising the information, including putting aside some contributions as not being of immediate relevance, although still of value.

B. Circle Time

'Circle time' is common practice in many classrooms. It gives children a sense of being valued equally, and develops support amongst themselves and between them and their leader; a sense of belonging. It helps children to:

- Concentrate on an idea, concept or topic;
- Listen;
- Think;
- Contribute.

Guidelines for circle time:

- Give pupils time to think before the session begins so they can focus their thoughts and plan their comments.
- Pupils remain seated in the place they chose at the start.
- Comments need to be positive and true.
- Children should feel it is "OK" to remain silent.
- Children only talk when it is their turn. A prop (symbolic microphone) passed round the circle reminds each child when it is his/her turn to speak.
- Each person listens to the person who is speaking.

C. Discussion

'Discussion' is a means of exploring ideas and concepts. It teaches pupils to listen, to express themselves, to follow and then to add to or refute a point. It helps develop opinions and broadens outlook. Everyone can contribute.

Suggested ground rules:

- You might want to use a symbolic microphone, e.g. a ruler, which is passed to the pupil who is to speak.
- Each person should finish speaking before moving on to the next speaker.
- You can disagree with someone's idea, but do so without attacking the person.
- Speak from your own experience or say where you got the idea from, e.g. TV, parents.
- You don't have to speak.
- Remember there may be more than one right answer.
- Ask for suggestions about additional ground rules.
- Reach agreement on the ground rules and abide by them.
- Display the rules.

D. Using role play

Role play provides a very direct way of examining alternative viewpoints or being able to look at an issue without people's own experiences being directly referred to.

Role play does not require acting skills, putting on a 'voice' or 'emoting', but it does require presenting someone else's point of view. Each role play has the same elements:

- An initial scenario;

- Background information which helps the participants understand their roles;

- Comment out of role;

- A principal learning aim which relates to real life.

A number of the activities in **Time for Rights** provide role play scenarios that describe some of the most worrying issues with which a child may be faced. Using role play allows children to explore these issues and help find solutions, without exposing their own personal experiences.

Your pupils may want to act out their role play. They may also need frequent careful interventions and steering to stimulate their imaginations and keep them on track.

Encourage them to spend a little time reading and discussing their role play situation before going into the role play. The role plays in this book provide scenarios and suggested 'conversations' for exploring the issue through role play, rather than providing information for several characters. Therefore, pupils have the freedom to present the discussions in several different ways without pre-given view-points.

For example, in Unit 3, activity 5 **Tell someone**, a scenario is given, then it is suggested that certain characters have a conversation about it, without these characters' viewpoints being pre-determined, i.e. pupils decide for themselves how Lisa's mother will react.

Lisa is seven years old. Several nights a week she is looked after by Marie who is a lot older than her. Sometimes Marie is kind and plays with Lisa, but when her boyfriend, John, comes round, Marie is quite nasty to Lisa. She makes Lisa go in her bedroom even when it's not bedtime. If Lisa comes out, Marie or John shout at her, and once John hit her quite hard.

Lisa told her aunt Hazel. What happens when Hazel tells Lisa's mother?

E. Presentations

Making a presentation is a feature of everyday life. New concepts and ideas have to be presented to individuals, a team or a large audience. A 'sell' of ideas or products is done either face to face or over the telephone. Despite all the new technology, the oral presentation is very much a part of the modern working environment. OHPs and Powerpoint serve as visual aids but are no substitute for the fluent, succinct spoken word. It is never too early to start developing vocabularly and oral skills.

1. **Introduction/beginning:** Why the subject was chosen?

2. **Middle:** The body of the subject: verbal description of an object or topic, how it is used/applied, the implications of any research that has been done and what is be done about it.

3. **Conclusion/end:** Summary of what has been learned/conclusions drawn.

Step 1: Preparation

- Research the topic/find the object;

- Prepare a draft... become familiar with the content;

- Rehearse the presentation out loud – see the three stages above;

- Time it;

- Amend the draft to fit allotted time span;

- Highlight key words;

- Write key sentences on individual cards and number the cards in case they are dropped;

- Memorise opening words and concluding sentence.

Step 2: Delivery

- Stand straight and still;

- Look pleasantly at the audience, making eye contact with individual members;

- Speak clearly and with appropriate volume so everybody can hear;

- Bring notes to chest height for easy reference, i.e. look down as little as possible;

- Notes should/can be, one or two word prompts, written extra large so they can be easily read from a distance;

- Do not read the notes verbatim;

- Do not put your hands anywhere near your face;

- Gradually increase the length of presentations.

Creating a cooperative classroom

Children have a right to freely express an opinion in all matters affecting them, and to have that opinion taken into account (Article 12).
All rights belong to all children...(Article 2).

First and foremost PSHE/PSE/PSD and Citizenship education require a classroom where all pupils feel they can contribute without fear of being mocked or denigrated. It takes time to build up a fully supportive climate. If your class is contentious, disruptive or ridden by factions, then much of this work may seem impossible because the environment will not be calm and friendly, and pupils will not dare to contribute opinions and experiences which are important to them.

The 'conflict resolution' activities suggested here may help to create the climate needed to proceed on to similarly structured activities in the Units. The two sessions described here use a technique widely used in developing countries to involve people in schemes that will help improve their communities. The method enables pupils to put their gripes and complaints on the table, have them discussed, reach an acceptable resolution, and then the class is able to move on.

The activities are designed to:

- Improve pupils' relationships with each other;

- Make speaking and listening activities worthwhile and enjoyable for everyone;

- Help pupils to be articulate and fluent.

You may want pupils to record some of their experiences and describe how they feel about them, while the work is in progress, so **diary** writing tasks are suggested.

Session 1 - What's preventing cooperation?

Objective: To provide a supportive environment for pupils to express their opinions about the class and its behaviour, and to have them listened to, with the long-term objective of improving pupils' behaviour.

Introduction

Tell the class you are going to do a piece of work which should make everyone in the class happier. They are going to look at the conflict/problems in their classroom. Ask the class how they would define 'conflict'.
You need to establish that:

- Physical conflict is harmful and destructive, and unacceptable anywhere;

- Verbal conflict can be just as harmful and destructive as physical violence;

- Conflicts of ideas and principles, which would be expressed orally or in writing, can be immensely constructive and bring about social and legal change.

Materials: Sufficient Index (3″ x 5″) cards, large Post-its or pieces of paper for students to write on, adhesive, drawing pins.

Activity

- Give every pupil a piece of card/paper or a large Post-it and ask them to write, in silence, one thing they think is wrong with the behaviour in the class. Assure them that their answers, no matter how critical, are wanted. This activity is anonymous, so they should not show their card to anyone and they can disguise their handwriting if they want. They do not sign their name.

- Go round and collect the cards. Shuffle them so they are not in any order.

- Read each answer aloud and then lay it on a flat surface or pin it on a board.

- Encourage your pupils to help you place the cards, clustering those which are similar.

- When all the responses are up you will have a number of small and large clusters of cards which map the class's problems.

- Invite your pupils to suggest any other problems that have not emerged. (These can again be done anonymously on cards, or maybe pupils will happily say them and you can write these each on a card and add it to the cards on the board.)

- Draw a bubble round each cluster and ask the class to try to give the cluster a title.

- Pupils then try to 'rank' these titles/problems:

  - In order of importance in terms of what is most disruptive;

  - The order in which they should to be tackled.

Written work or homework

This can be a diary entry in which pupils describe:

- The problems the class is having;

- What they, personally, did in the lesson;

- How they felt during and after the session;

- Their hopes for the next session.

Session 2 - Solving problems

Objective: To build on the pupil's understanding of conflict/the problems in their classroom; for them to participate in finding ways of dealing with it.

Materials: Sufficient Index cards, large Post-its or pieces of paper for students to write, adhesive, drawing pins.

Activity

- Explain that today you are going to look at ways of solving the problems identified in the last session.

- Give out cards and pupils write on each one a solution to one behaviour problem, using as many cards as they wish. Again, the answer is confidential.

- Read each answer aloud and group them, with the pupils' help.

- Draw a bubble round each cluster and ask the class to try to give the cluster a title.

- Invite your pupils to suggest any other solutions that have not emerged.

- Look at your list of problems from the previous activity. Can the solutions be matched to the problems?

- Ask pupils what might be the greatest problem with trying to put the solutions into practice - record all their answers.

Decide on what solutions the class will try to take forward.

Written work or homework

- Pupils write sentences or a paragraph about how the solutions were agreed on, and what their reaction was to any of them.

- Pupils each make one resolve about their own behaviour which will help bring about a change in the classroom.

Session 3 – Building cooperation

Objective: To introduce pupils to cooperation building activities.

Materials: Five to eight scarves for blindfolds.

Activity

Use the hall or move the tables/desks to the side of the classroom and place the chairs in a circle. Lay out some of the furniture as an obstacle course.

- Ask for six volunteers to make their way round the obstacle course blindfolded. Blindfold all except one.

- Each volunteer puts their hands on the shoulders of the person in front of them. The person who can see stands at the back. Explain that they are not allowed to talk to each other but must use non-verbal means of communication.

- The group is allowed a brief discussion to work out a non-verbal code of communication (give examples only if you think it's necessary, e.g. tap on left shoulder means one step left, etc.).

- The group make their way round the obstacle course, guided by the sighted person at the rear. The rest of the class watch.

- Let the blindfolded and the sighted person explain what the experience felt like.

If possible, repeat the activity until all have taken part.

Variation:
- Work in pairs, one sighted person leading a blindfolded person. Several groups could do this at the same time.

Written work or homework
- Pupils write about the day's session and how they felt taking part in the cooperation activity.

- Pupils also write about their hopes for the class's future.

Learning to mediate

Many schools are introducing peer mediation programmes to help them solve disuputes in the playground and among pupils. This is a highly skilled process and there are a number of organisations which undertake this in schools. See Resources, page 126, for some addresses.

Glossary

We suggest that all pupils need to know and understand these words or terms.

Active listening
A communication skill in which the listener paraphrases the speaker, reflects the speaker's feelings, asks open questions to elicit information and checks to see s/he has heard the speaker correctly.

Affirmation (building self-esteem)
The recognition and expression of strengths, skills, value, qualities, positive behaviours, or positive efforts, either in oneself or in others. Affirmation, when given genuinely, helps to build a positive self-image and mutual respect.

Assertiveness
A way of communicating in situations of conflict or potential conflict, which involves both the honest expression of feelings and needs, and respect for the rights of the other person.

Bias
Holding fixed opinions or to have a tendency in favour of or against something, without knowing enough to be able to judge.

Communicate
To make opinions, feelings and information known or understood by others in speech, writing, body movement, etc.

Conflict
A state of disagreement or argument between opposing groups or opposing ideas and principles held by others.

Conflict resolution
Explores the ways in which conflict and controversy may be tackled. The skills are non-confrontational, non-violent and can be used to solve disputes anytime, e.g. personal disputes, in the family, in class and further a field.

Cooperate
To work together for a shared purpose.

Discrimination
To treat someone 'less favourably' than another on racial, sexual, cultural or religious grounds. (Prejudice put into action.)

Effective listening
The recognition that one has been truly heard, or has truly heard someone else, especially in a time of conflict.

Mediation
Using a neutral third party to assist those in conflict come to a mutually agreed resolution. Mediator - the neutral person acting as a peacemaker between those holding opposing viewpoints.

NGOs
Non-governmental organisations, e.g. Childline, Save the Children, UNICEF in the UK. (Overseas UNICEF is an intergovernmental organisation.)

Prejudice
Actions, feelings or opinions formed or undertaken without sufficiently informed thought or knowledge. Often called 'blind prejudice', i.e. the person cannot 'see', or does not want to see, without bias.

Problem solving
Brain-storming/thought-showering/list and discuss, can be the first step in problem solving. Pupils are asked to think of as many ideas or solutions as they can, and all answers are accepted. Pupils review the options, discard those they think are unworkable, and decide on the best possible solution/s to the problem.

Racism
The belief that racial differences between people are the influence on their characters and abilities - believing that ones own race is superior; dislike or unfair treatment of people based on their race, culture or religion.

Rights
Those things that are fair and just for all people throughout the world to possess, which are essential to a person's freedom, well being and dignity and which are recognised by all and underpinned by law.

Stereotype
A fixed set of ideas about what a particular type of 'person' or 'thing' is like, which is (wrongly) believed to be true in all cases.

What are childrens' rights?

Activities to introduce children to the rights in the United Nations Convention on the Rights of the Child.

Activities will help your pupils:

- Differentiate between a 'want' and a 'need' and learn that basic needs should be met by right;

- Come to a realisation that rights bring responsibilities;

- Recognise that for everyone to enjoy their rights sometimes means compromise;

- See how children's rights can be applied to children's problems, through consideration of other children's problems;

- Realise that abuses of children's rights often need help from outside agencies, which are there to help them;

- Realise that children all over the world have these rights, and are using them as active citizens;

- Practice expressing their own point of view and listening to other people's.

Articles in the UN Convention on the Rights of the Child relevant to Unit 1:

- The right to know about the Convention (Article 42).

- All children have these rights (Article 2).

- Children have the right to meet together and to join groups and organisations (Article 15).

- Children with a disability have the right to special care and support (Article 23).

- Children's right to government support to their families/carers (Articles 18, 20, 26 and 27).

- Protection from sexual abuse, drug abuse and violence (Articles 19, 33, 34).

N.B. Background information on the United Nations Convention on the Rights of the Child can be found on pages 5-12.

Wants and needs

Objective: For pupils to learn to differentiate between a 'want' and a 'need'.

Materials: Working in pairs or groups, each group needs a set of the 'Wants and needs' cards (photocopied from pages 29-32) and pre-cut, or you can buy sets of the cards in different colours from UNICEF (see Resources page 126), a large sheet of paper and adhesive. You need to ensure that each pair has four blank cards on which they can add their own 'want' or 'need'. Each group will need space to lay the cards out.

This is of role-play exercise in which a 'group of important adults' are the decisions makers. The words in italics are suggested text to read to your pupils.

Introduction

Give out the Wants and needs cards to each group. Ask pupils to spread them out so they can see them all.

Activity

Teacher: "A group of important adults have realised that children need certain things as they grow up. The pictures on these cards represent the things they would like to make sure all children have."

- Ask your pupils to add four items that they think are missing on the blank cards.

- After a few minutes explain that, "For economic reasons the adults have decided they can provide young people with only 16 items so you must decide which eight items you are willing to give up."

- Inform them they have five minutes to decide. The cards each pair discards should be collected up.

- When you have collected the discarded cards tell your pupils, "Further cuts are needed and you must discard another eight cards."

- Give them 5 – 10 minutes to discard another eight cards, which you collect.

- Pupils stick their remaining cards onto the paper.

Plenary

Discuss which items were most commonly eliminated in the first round and why.

- Ask pairs if they had any disagreements over the items to eliminate. Which ones, and why?

Hopefully words like 'need' and 'want' or 'essential' and 'inessential' will come out in the discussion.

- Discuss the difference between a 'want' and a 'need'.

- See if the class can come up with definitions for 'wants' and 'needs'.

Wants and needs

Further discussion

- Explain that children have a right to have their basic needs met because of the UN Convention on the Rights of the Child that all countries in the world have signed, except two – Somalia and the USA*. Provide copies of the Convention to each child or group. Copies can be either the summary of the Convention on pages 7-8, or copies of the "What Rights?" leaflet. (A summary of the Convention especially for children available FREE from UNICEF – see Resources page 126.)

- Does the rest of the world agree with you? Pupils compare their 8 'needs' cards with the 'rights' that children have?

- Pupils draw up their own list of basic rights for people of their age.

Extension activities

Writing

- 'What I have learned about 'wants, needs and rights'.

- Class or group discussion to formulate a definition of a right.

Discussion or group activity

- Do wants and needs differ for different people? Why? Why not?

- Do all groups in society get their needs and wants met equally?

- If not, what accounts for the differences?

- Is it fair that inequalities exist?

* Somalia has not ratified the Convention because it is not a unified country and does not have one government. The USA has signed that it will ratify but has not yet ratified; its federal system making it difficult for a decision to be made on behalf of all states.

Nutritious food

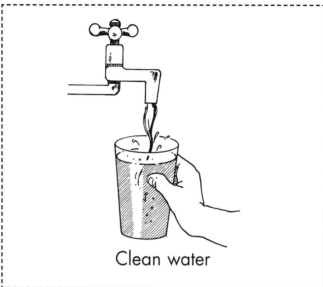

Clean water

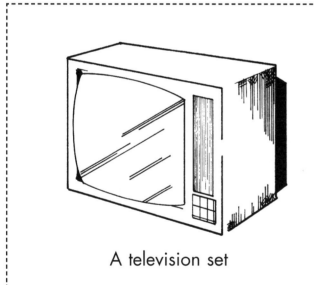

A television set

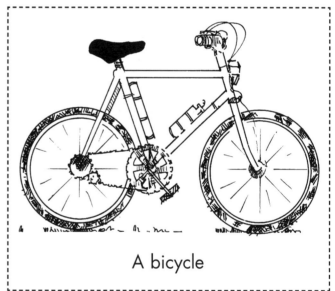

A bicycle

The opportunity to express your opinion and be listened to

Medical care when you need it

Your own bedroom

Fast food

Protection from discrimination

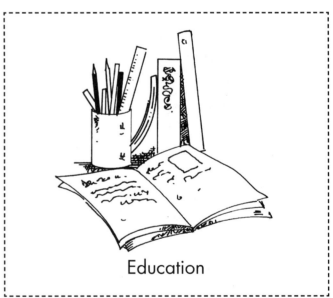

Education

Money to spend as you like

Holiday trips

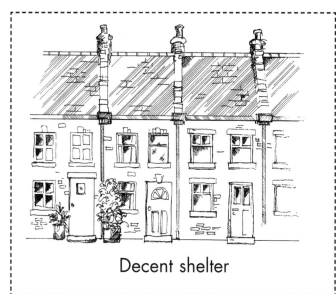

Decent shelter

The opportunity to practise
your own religion and culture

A personal computer

Clothes in the latest style

Clean air

Protection from abuse and neglect

Wants and needs cards

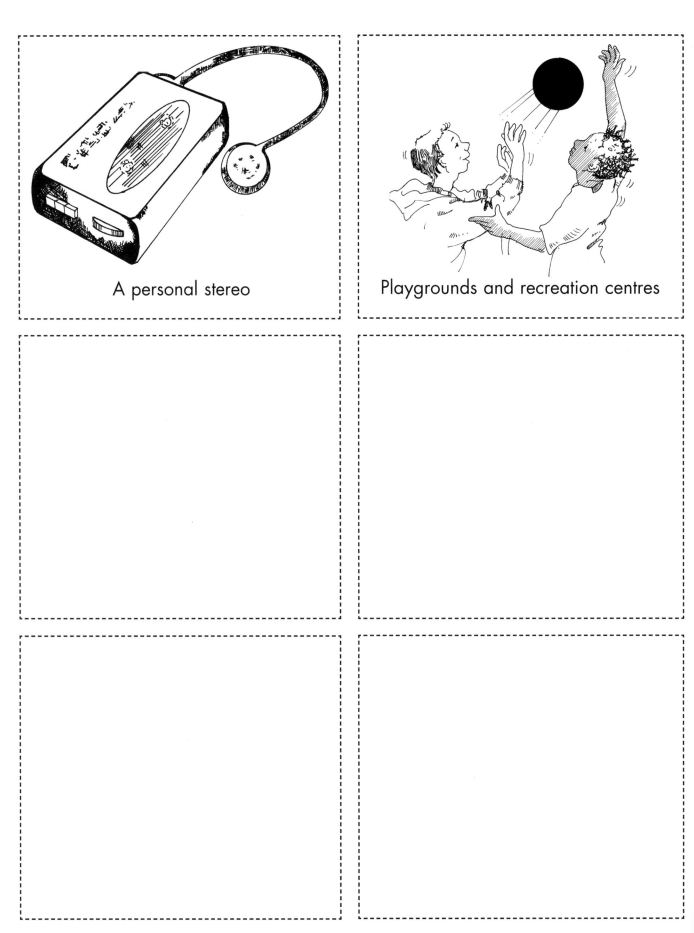

A personal stereo

Playgrounds and recreation centres

"I've got rights........ and responsibilities!"

Objective: To help pupils understand that if they have rights they also have responsibilities.

Materials: Copies of the **"I've got rights!"** and **"I've got responsibilities!"** pages 34 & 35 for each pair of pupils in the class who is going to participate. Plain paper to cut into cards.

Introduction

List and discuss the rights which children everywhere should have. If you have completed activity 1.1 Wants and needs, you may have already done this.

Give pairs of pupils either a copy of "I've got rights!" or a copy of "I've got responsibilities!", pages 34 & 35. (Cards 8 and H are already blank for pupils to make their own rights and responsibilities.)

Tell them to read all the statements through, then, on separate pieces of paper, to make up reciprocating 'rights' or 'responsibilities' to match their cards.

Activity

Pupils then pair up – those with rights pages with those with responsibility pages. They compare their own 'rights' and 'responsibilities' with those on the cards. (At this point they may need to cut the printed pages into cards.)

Alternatively this could be done as a class with pairs reading out their 'rights' and 'responsibilities' and matching them with the printed cards.

Pupils also share their own 'right' for number 8, and appropriate 'responsibility' (H) to match it.

Alternative activity – could be a homework activity pupils do with parents

● Pupils are given copies of the two pages 34 & 35 and told to match them by cutting up the cards from the "I've got responsibilities!" sheet and placing the appropriate card alongside the matching 'right'.

● They complete no.8 with another right that they consider important and then a matching 'responsibility' (card H).

● Cards are laid on the larger sheet of paper and glued.

● Pupils bring them into school and share not only their findings but also their parents' reactions.

Plenary

Pupils share a right they wrote themselves with the class, other circle members then suggest the matching responsibility.

Answers: 1-B, 2-E, 3-F, 4-C, 5-D, 6-A, 7-G, 8-H.

1. Children have the right to be looked after by doctors and nurses...

2. All children have the right to express their opinion...

3. Children have the right to a good school...

4. Children have the right to be protected and looked after...

5. Children have the right to a safe and comfortable home...

6. Children have the right to be proud of where they come from and what they believe in...

7. Children have the right to be well fed...

8. Children have the right to...

"I've got responsibilities!"

A. ...and everyone has the responsibility to respect where people come from and what they believe in.

B. ...and everyone has the responsibility to help others have good health.

C. ...and everyone has the responsibility not to hurt others.

D. ...and everyone has the responsibility to make sure all children have homes.

E. ...and everyone has the responsibility to listen to others.

F. ...and everyone has the responsibility to work as well as they are able.

G. ...and everyone has the responsibility to prevent people from starving.

H. ...and everyone has the responsibility to ...

1.3   ## The Rights Path

Objective: To build on the previous activities and for pupils to demonstrate an understanding of rights and responsibilities in action.

Materials: Copies of the cartoon story, **The Rights Path** (page 37).

Introduction

Share the story in The Rights Path and discuss what it means.

Activity

Working in groups, pupils could bring this story to life in one of several ways:

- Dramatise the story and perform it to the class.

- Make up their own version of the story, either to dramatise or to write, to illustrate the message of the need to compromise if everyone's rights are to be respected.

- It could be mimed by a group with a narrator.

- It could be done as a series of freeze frames with a narration per freeze.

Plenary

- Pupils discuss the reciprocal nature of having rights and responsibilities, and what this means for their own behaviour in the classroom and towards others.

- How does this knowledge about rights and responsibilities make them feel about themselves, about other children, about adults?

Examples of children's rights in action around the world can be found throughout the book.

1.4   What rights do they need?

Objective: For pupils to see that all children have all rights, without exception.

Materials: Bega's Story page 39, **What rights do they need? Story cards** page 40, **Rights cards** page 41. Prepare the cards for the way you want to use them.

Introduction

Read or tell your pupils the first story from the Story cards, which is about Bega. Ask them what rights he needed to have met, use the Rights cards to help pupils select rights.

Then read or tell the full story about Bega on page 39, to show how his rights were met when he went to Casa Grande. This story shows how when children's rights are not being met, outsiders can help. The first step to taking action is to recognise that all children have the rights they have learned about, and if one of these rights is not being met or abused then they should seek help.

Activity

With pupils working in groups, give each group one or more of the Story cards and a sheet of the Rights cards, which they could cut up if it helps. Pupils need to show which rights should apply.

Plenary

Pupils share their findings and discuss.

- The class could then look at one or more of the stories and talk about how that child, and/or his or her family, could go about getting the help they need.

Extension activity

Pupils could write and ask for information on what different organisations are doing to ensure that children are given their rights, e.g. Save the Children, UNICEF, NSPCC, National Children's Bureau, Childline (see Resources page 127 for addresses).

- Pupils write a story or prepare a dramatisation of their own example, real or imaginary, of a child that needs some of his or her rights met.

This activity can be linked to the timeline activity in Unit 2.6 (pages 55-56), when pupils could consider what outside organisations, or people, may help them in the future.

Bega's story - Brazil

Bega was born blind. For the first 15 years of his life he had no special care or education to help him live his life. His days were bleak and empty. All he could do was lie in his hammock and wait for his brothers to come home from school and include him in their play. And it was one of his brothers, Alexandre, who helped change Bega's life.

Alexandre had started to come to an arts centre for children, Casa Grande, which had opened in their town. One day, Alexandre took Bega along. Since he came over a year ago, Bega has learned to play the guitar, harmonica and keyboard. He sings and performs like a professional. He also has his own radio programme on the radio station the centre has started. He has labelled all the CDs he likes to play so he can find them on his own. Soon he will go to the city of Fortaleza for a year to learn braille and skills to help him live a full life. Then he will return and teach other blind children at Casa Grande. He also hopes to be a musician and composer.

Before he came to Casa Grande Bega's future was bleak. He had few friends and no independence; his future would have been as a beggar. Now he has friends, many skills and interests, and a future.

What rights do they need? Story cards

Match the Rights cards to the Story cards below. Rights can be used as many times as necessary and children can have more than one right.

1. Bega has been blind since birth. Since he is blind he doesn't go to the local school. All he does all day is hang around waiting until his brothers come home from school and play with him.

2. Jamie is one year old. He has had health problems since birth. This is not helped by the fact that his home is damp and his parents are unemployed and so have little money for extra food and medicines.

3. Zlata is ten years old. She came to England from Romania two years ago with her married sister, but she wishes her mum and dad could come. Every time they try to enter the country they are sent back.

4. Liam is eight years old. His family live on the sixth floor. Liam loves playing football but the playground by his flats is often occupied by bigger boys who threaten him.

5. Natalie is frightened at school because of the gangs, and she's frightened where she lives because of the drug dealers that hang around the local shops. Natalie wants to do well at school and join a group with other children like herself who care about things.

6. Jackie is 11 years old. Her stepbrother keeps coming into her bedroom at night. She is worried about becoming pregnant, but she doesn't know the facts of life. Jackie wants help but she's too frightened to tell her mum.

Rights cards

Right to education.
Article 28

Right to an opinion.
Article 12

Right to live with your family.
Article 10

Right to play and leisure.
Article 31

Right to information.
Article 13

Right of children with disabilities to support so they can lead a full life.
Article 23

Right to equal rights, whoever you are, wherever you live.
Article 22

Right to be protected from sexual abuse.
Article 34

Right to be protected from dangerous drugs.
Article 33

Right to healthcare.
Article 24

Right to be protected from violence.
Article 19

Right to a decent standard of living.
Article 27

Objective: To understand that children's rights are universal and that in other countries they are taken very seriously and children are listened to. This can be linked to **Running a Campaign** in Unit 5.5.

Materials: a ball of wool or string.

Introduction

- **Display the Colombian Peace Constructor badge and ask them what they think it might mean.**

- **Read them the story of the Children's Movement for Peace and discuss what happened.**

Activities

Play the activity Farlis describes in the story:

- Ask pupils to stand in a circle.

- Pupils throw the ball of wool or string from person to person.

- When they catch the ball, each pupil says a right that they think needs more attention in their school or community.

- With a large group each child only has one go, but with a small group each child could have several goes.

    Or

- Pupils make badges with a message, e.g. anti-bullying badges.

- Pupils make a list of things they would like to try and see change in school, the community or further afield.

- Pick one issue from the list that they would like to campaign about.

Plenary

- Discuss the activity and the story, and talk about the problems the children of Colombia may have had to face to organise their ballot.

- Refer to rights and responsibilities and apply these to the story – the right for peace and the responsibility to try to bring it about.

- What were the main issues your pupils brought forward when they played the activity with the string?

- Display the badges.

- Discuss the list of campaigning issues.

Children's Movement for Peace - Colombia

In Colombia a war has been going on for more than forty years. It is a brutal conflict between many different armed groups who struggle for control over land and power. About five thousand people are killed every year in the war and most of these are civilians.

Since 1985, more than two million people, many of them children and their families, have been forced to abandon their homes and go to live elsewhere, sometimes to live in a camp like refugees. Even more people become victims of the general violence of the society. Children whose lives have been turned upside down by the violence, drop out of schools and join gangs.

By 1996, many young people decided that they could not bear to live in such a violent country. They organised a children's election across the whole of Colombia. Children voted for the human rights which were most important to them. Nearly three million children voted overwhelmingly for peace.

Farlis was 15 years old when she started to work for peace. She went to a workshop for children and adults trying to do something about the violence. She says:

"We played a game. We stood in a circle and threw a ball of string to each other. Every person who caught the ball had to describe something they would do to help make peace. Every time they threw the ball the string unravelled but everyone who had caught the ball kept hold of the string so that by the end of the game we had formed a giant web with the string. We pulled and tugged at the web and found it was very strong. We learned that if we worked together, if we formed a web like that, we could have a much greater impact."

The Children's Movement helped to lay the foundation for peace in communities, schools and families, which is essential if a political solution to end the violence is to be found.

Farlis (left) and fellow peace activists.

Everyone should know about children's rights

This section suggests other ways children can be actively engaged in telling others about children's rights.

- Using sheet **You might not know this** (page 45) pupils could dramatise/do freeze frames/mime, etc. for presentation to the school.

- Pupils make their own pictures/collage/frieze using **You might not know this** with groups working on different aspects of the Convention and rights.

- Pupils compile a number of assemblies based on the actvities and stories in this Unit. Assemblies or performances could take many forms, e.g. dramatisations, radio or television interview, presentations with readings, music and speeches.

- Pupils plan for the school to celebrate International Children's Rights Day on 20 November – **Running a campaign**, Unit 5.5, might help.

Research

UNICEF's website **Voices of Youth** has interactive activities about children's rights that your pupils can use, enjoy and learn from. These pictures *Pictures from internet* can be found on: http://www.unicef.org/voy/meeting/rig/rigpics.html

Other websites: www.savethechildren.org.uk/rightonline/index.html (Save the Children's young people's web pages), www.therightssite.org.uk (UNICEF's young people's website), www.globalgang, (Christian Aid's young people's website), www.oxfam.org.uk/coolplanet/kidsweb/what.htm (Oxfam's young people's website).

Homework

You might not know this (page 45) and **The Rights Path** (page 37) could be taken home to be shared with carers.

- Pupils ask several adults of different ages what it was like being a child, when they were the same age as your pupils. Ask them to find out things like:
- How were they treated?
- How were they punished?
- Did adults listen to them?
- What did they like to do best?
- Did they like school?

Pupils could agree a list of things to ask before undertaking the homework.

YOU MIGHT NOT KNOW THIS

BUT EVERY CHILD IN THE WORLD HAS RIGHTS. THESE ARE THE THINGS WE NEED TO GROW UP SAFE, HAPPY AND HEALTHY.

SO THE LITTLE BOY FORCED TO WORK IN A GRIM BURMESE FACTORY...

THE TEENAGE GIRL BULLIED IN A POSH KENYAN SCHOOL...

AND THE GUY BORN WITH SPINA BIFIDA IN AN ORDINARY SUBURB OF NEW YORK...

ALL HAVE THE SAME RIGHTS AS WE DO.

YOU COULD LEAD A LIFE OF LUXURY, SURROUNDED BY EVERYTHING YOU WANT, AND STILL HAVE RIGHTS THAT ARE WRONGED. EVERY DAY ADULTS MAKE DECISIONS THAT AFFECT CHILDREN.

YEH, BUT WHEN WAS THE LAST TIME THEY ASKED OUR OPINION AND TOOK IT SERIOUSLY?

MOST RIGHTS ARE SIMPLER, LIKE THE RIGHT TO PLAY, TO BE TAKEN CARE OF, TO HAVE FRIENDS...

BUT IN MANY COUNTRIES THESE ARE LUXURIES CHILDREN CAN ONLY DREAM ABOUT.

SO, IN 1989, THE UNITED NATIONS GOT THE WORLD TO SIGN UP TO THE CONVENTION ON THE RIGHTS OF THE CHILD [C.R.C]. ONLY TWO COUNTRIES HAVEN'T.

GETTING 191 COUNTRIES TO ACTUALLY CHANGE THEIR WAYS AND RECOGNISE THE RIGHTS OF CHILDREN ISN'T EASY SO, EVERY FIVE YEARS, THE PROGRESS OF GOVERNMENT IS CHECKED ON OUR BEHALF.

OUR RIGHTS ARE LISTED IN 42 ARTICLES, BUT WE CAN'T EXPECT ADULTS TO RESPECT THESE RIGHTS IF WE DON'T RESPECT THE RIGHTS OF EACH OTHER.

JULIE SINCLAIR '00

What do rights mean to me?

Activities to help children recognise that each has a unique identity which should be valued.

Activities will help your pupils:

- Value themselves and others, and recognise that everyone has the right to feel good about themselves;

- Understand the importance of individual identity and that we should respect each other's differences;

- Realise the importance of birth registration for recognition of existence by governments;

- Consider the future and the possibilities it offers;

- Recognise that every child has a place in the world and that they all want and need the same things.

Articles in the UN Convention on the Rights of the Child relevant to Unit 2:

- All children have rights (Article 2).

- The right to an identity (Article 7).

- Government respect of children's right to a name, nationality and family ties (Article 8).

- The right to get and share information, as long as the information is not damaging to them or others (Article 13).

I am special

Objective: Pupils realise that everyone has a completely different identity and that each one of us is unique (special).

Materials: Pencil, paper or **I am special** (page 48), each child brings a photograph of themselves.

Introduction

List and discuss or thought-shower what makes each one of them special, e.g. features, talents, family name, family traditions etc. to collect appropriate vocabulary. If relevant, read and discuss I am special.

Activity

- Working independently, pupils list all the things which they think constitute their identity and make them unique (special), e.g. their name, family name, family features and characteristics, personality traits etc.

- Pupils share their lists with their neighbour and, if necessary, add to their lists.

- Pupils complete I am special using either a drawing or a photograph of themselves and picking some of the things they listed which they think constitute their identity.

Plenary

- Pupils in groups choose one person's 'identity list' to read out and the rest of the class guess who the person is.

- Each child makes a passport, or make a display of the completed **I am special** sheets.

Circle time

- Pupils each make a positive remark to their neighbour and the reason for this remark.

Writing

- Each child writes a description of why they are liked, using the positive remarks from circle time.

I am special

Put a picture of yourself in the middle rectangle, and write the reasons you are special in the blank shapes.

....

is special because

....

....

Identity show and tell

Objective: Pupils talk about their family identity, and develop their oral/presentation skills.

Materials: Each pupil needs to bring to school an artefact associated with their family. Optional - **My family artefact** (page 56).

Introduction

Talk about 'giving talks' or 'presentations' (see Teachers Notes page 19), and go through the procedure that you expect them to follow:

- **A brief verbal description of the object;**

- **Where it comes from and who in the family it belongs to;**

- **Why they have brought it to talk about;**

- **Why they consider it an important part of their family's identity.**

Activity

- Pupils help each other to prepare a talk about their artefact using the above or similar brief.

- Pupils give their presentations to either a small group or the whole class. The listeners then asks questions about the artefact.

Plenary

- Discuss the artefacts pupils brought in. Do they have anything in common? What parts of ourselves, our family and our culture seem to make the most impact?

- Pupils could complete **My family artefact,** or draw their artefact and write a sentence about it.

Extension activity

Identity collage

Pupils bring their own family photographs, magazine pictures, newspaper clippings, small objects, etc. to create a collage about themselves, their family and cultural identity. These collages could be displayed as an exhibition to which other classes, parents, governors, etc. are invited. Pupils conduct their visitors around the exhibition.

(Obviously you will need to take care that the pupils' artefacts are safe at all times.)

My family artefact

Name ....Date ....

Fill in the answers to these questions:

What is the artefact called? ....

Where did it come from? ....

Who does it belong to? ....

How long has the family had it? ....

How did the family get it? ....

Where is it kept? ....

What does it tell us about your family? ....

Why did you choose it? ....

Use the answers above to help you prepare the information to put beside your artefact.

This is a ....

It comes from ....

It belongs to ....

We have had it ....

We keep it ....

I chose it because ....

Helping others feel good

Objective: To let the pupils feel positive about themselves and to assess the positive qualities in their peers.

Materials: A4 paper and pencil for every child.

Introduction

Remind the children how they have learned about how they are all unique and how wonderful this is. Talk about how we all like to receive praise and how they did this in circle time (page 47).

It may be prudent to keep those who are antagonistic towards each other apart.

Activity

- Pupils work in groups of five. Each child has a sheet of A4 paper and a pencil.

- Pupils write their name at the top of the paper and draw round their hand.

- Then they pass their sheet to the person sitting on their right.

- When the next pupil receives their neighbour's drawing, they write a word or phrase about that person in one of the fingers. The comment about the person must be true, kind and important.

- Continue to pass the drawings until each pupil gets their own sheet back again.

- Pupils read the comments about themselves.

For less able pupils, this activity could be preceded by a discussion of appropriate vocabulary for them to draw upon when doing the activity.

Plenary

Discuss and do the following:

- Did you enjoy this activity. Why? Why not?

- What have you learned from this activity?

- Pupils record the comments and or their feelings about the comments.

- Each pupil states something they have learned about themselves.

- Discuss and make a list of the ways pupils and teacher can help each member of the class feel 'good' about themselves.

- Display the list of suggestions.

- Pupils start trying to make the ideas work.

- Review their progress weekly.

2.4   Name or number?

Objective: To experience being called a number and to appreciate the value of having a name. Also, by recording their feelings throughout the day, they experience the personal benefits of keeping a diary.

Materials: A large label for each child with assorted numbers, e.g. 99, 151, 298, 333, 793, 1000, 1976, etc

Introduction

- Inform the school that your pupils are each going to wear a number for the day and that number will be their name for the day.

- Ask pupils and teachers to help by calling your class members by their number, when they speak to them in the playground, at lunch, etc.

- Explain to the class that for a day they are going to experience being known by a number and not by their name.

- Give each pupil a large number to wear for the day.

Activity

- Pupils keep a diary of the day, in which, at set times, they record their feelings about the experiences and incidents that occur.

- Entry 1: On receiving their number, pupils write a short paragraph about what difference this might make to their day.

- Entry 2: Could be immediately after morning break when others outside their class have also used their number instead of their name.

- Entry 3: Could be after lunch.

- Entry 4: Could be after afternoon break – just before you end the activity.

Plenary

- At the end of the day let the children take off their numbers. Ask them what happened and how they feel about their experiences during the day.

- A vote could be taken on whether or not they enjoyed the activity. Would they recommend it to other children?

- Were there numbers they would have preferred to have had, or not had? Why?

- What do they now feel about their names? Are names important? Why? Why not?

The importance of birth registration

Objective: For pupils to realise that in the UK births are registered, and that this means that you exist and are entitled to things like healthcare and education. However, in many countries this does not automatically happen and many children in the world have difficulties, because, as far as the state is concerned, they do not exist.

Materials: The boy without a birth certificate (page 54). Sample birth certificate/s.

Introduction

Read **The boy without a birth certificate** to the class.

- **Discuss why a birth certificate is important, i.e. a person does not have rights if their name has not been officially documented.**

- **Clarify that pupils understand why Adin needed to have his birth registered.**

Activity

- In pairs or small groups, children make a list of question they would like to ask Adin.

Plenary

- Pupils share their questions with the class and display them.
- Reread them the story.
- Are their questions answered by the story?
- Can they hypothesise answers to any of their questions?
- Look at the sample birth certificate and explain what they are and why they are important.

Extension activity

Pupils could find out about laws for registering births in the United Kingdom, e.g. How do you know that a birth has to be registered? How many days do parents have to register a birth? What happens if a birth is not registered?

- You might like to ask your local registrar to talk with the class.

Adin is Romanian and his birth was not registered in the government records of births.

This meant that as a child he did not exist because the country had no record of his birth. He did not receive any of the childhood vaccinations against measles, polio or whooping cough. He cannot go to a doctor or go to school.

When Adin reaches the age of 14 he will need his birth certificate to get his "ID" (Identification card). Without this he will not be able to have a home, a job, use public transport, vote in elections or have a passport.

In the picture Adin (on the right, in the grey t-shirt) is nine years old, living in a children's home with his brother and five sisters.

Now Adin, and his brother and sisters, have birth certificates. The staff in the children's home where he is living managed to find his birth in hospital records. Once they found this information they asked the courts to give him a birth certificate. His brother and sisters' births had been registered in Germany, where his parents were living at the time.

Where am I going?

Objectives: For pupils to consider their futures.

Materials: Copies of **Views of the past and the future** (page 56). A drawing of a timeline on the board. Paper and pencils for pupils.

Introduction

Share the the views of children in Views of the past and the future and discuss them.

Activity

- Draw a timeline on the board for pupils to copy.

- Show pupils how to record significant events in their lives on the timeline, starting with their birth, then the most important events in their life so far. Then ask your pupils to think about the future and what they would like their life to be like when they are grown up.

- **Bega's Story,** from Unit 1 (page 39) could be referred to here. Born blind, he faces a fulfilling future because of help from his brother and a young person's organisation. Pupils could think about how other things may affect their future.

Extension activity

Time lines could be placed on display for children and parents to read.

Hans Christian Anderson's story "The Ugly Duckling", where an ugly duckling turns out to really be a beautiful swan, could be read or told to the class and pupils discuss:

- The meaning behind the story;

- The point/moral of the story;

- How they can apply it to their own lives.

This may be an ideal time to speak with each pupil about their potential and their worth as an individual.

Views of the past and the future

Views of the past

"Girls don't have to leave school now when they're 15 because their mothers don't have to teach them how to cook and clean while the men go out and get to work and pay the bills. It should be equal and they should both pay the bills."

Tehrim (10)

"They used to play kerby and hopscotch in the street. We still play these games today but not all the time. We play on the Playstation or computer games and watch TV."

Liam (8)

"Children used to get beaten when they were naughty. Now we get red cards and yellow cards."

Matthew (10)

"Before, ages ago, black people didn't get as good opportunities as the white people did, like white people got better jobs than they did. It's changing now but there are still a few racist people about, but it's changed a lot more than it used to be."

Naomi (10)

Views of the future

"I want to go to university and after that I will be a singer or a dancer. I want to be a football player and do gymnastics. I would like to live in Tenerife or Canada."

Nina (9)

"I will be trying to get a good job where I could try to get money so that I could look after my family. I would be a nurse if I had a chance to be."

Tanisha (9)

"I will be an actor or a singer with a flash car. I'll have two kids, one boy and one girl. I'll have a boyfriend but not a husband because they ruin your life. I will have a beautiful house in America. I will have lots of fans and be quite brainy."

Naomi (10)

"It's harder to get a job these days. For factory work you don't get that much money and if you've got a family it's even worse, but if you've got qualifications you've got a better chance. People want clever people like doctors and things like that. I want to be a doctor when I'm older."

Tehrim (10)

Young people's voices, London 2001

A place in the world for me

Objective: To explore and discuss the connections between people in the classroom and the wider world.

Materials: Simple world map, Post-it stickers sufficient for each pupil to have at least two stickers, atlases, tape or string.

Introduction

Talk to your pupils about how we all have links with different parts of the world and tell them that they are going to show that on the world map.

Activity

- Each pupil is to think about family and friends who don't currently live in the UK. They write down their names and the country where each relative or friend lives.

- Each pupil shares the information with another person/persons and then writes two of them down, each on their own sticker.

- The pupils tell each other as much as they know about this person and anything they know about the country

- Pupils use an atlas to find where these people live.

- Each pupil puts their Post-its on the appropriate country on the world map.

- Pupils could bring in photos of themselves, or with the family or friends who are now overseas and, using tape or string, link their portraits with the appropriate place on the world map.

Plenary

Discuss the extent of the global contacts that result. Let the pupils comment on the information gathered.

2.8 A right to be me

This section suggests ways children can actively share what they have learned about the importance of identity and of valuing themselves and others, and how this helps them find their place in the world.

- Much of the work on identity could be shared at assembly, i.e. some children could present their work on why they are special, some their family artefact, etc.

- Adin's story could be presented as a television interview. Then information about what we have that identifies us, i.e. birth certificate, passport etc. could be discussed.

- Children share how they felt while doing the 'name or number' activity (page 52) and their perceptions of why they think names, rather than numbers, are important.

- The story of Hans Christian Anderson's **The Ugly Duckling** (lyrics on page 59) could be dramatised for assembly.

- Pupils learn to sing the song **Naming of Children** using the **Thursday's Child Songbook** and perform it, they could also watch the video of **Thursday's Child**, particularly the section where the children are named.

Homework

- Pupils find out how their name was chosen and given to them.

- Pupils ask their parents if they can see documents that confirm their family's identity: birth certificate, marriage certificate, passport, driving licence etc.

- Pupils ask their parents what their hopes were for the future when they were at their age.

The Ugly Duckling

There once was an ugly duckling

With feathers all stubby and brown

And the other birds said in so many words

Get out of town

Get out, get out, get out of town

And he went with a quack and a waddle and a quack

In a flurry of eiderdown

That poor little ugly duckling

Went wandering far and near

But at every place they said to his face

Now get out, get out, get out of here

And he went with a quack and a waddle and a quack

And a very unhappy tear

All through the wintertime he hid himself away

Ashamed to show his face, afraid of what others might say

All through the winter in his lonely clump of wheat

Till a flock of swans spied him there and very soon agreed

You're a very fine swan indeed!

A swan? Me a swan? Ah, go on!

And he said yes, you're a swan

Take a look at yourself in the lake and you'll see

And he looked, and he saw, and he said

I am a swan! Wheeeeeeee!

I'm not such an ugly duckling

No feathers all stubby and brown

For in fact these birds in so many words said

The best in town, the best, the best

The best in town

Not a quack, not a quack, not a waddle or a quack

But a glide and a whistle and a snowy white back

And a head so noble and high

Say who's an ugly duckling?

Not I!

Not I!

What do rights mean in the family?

Activities to help children explore their need for, and right to, care and protection, and the roles of carers.

Activities will help your pupils:

- Realise that *families* take many shapes and forms, and all are acceptable if they care for children;

- Understand 'caring' relationships and where and how children fit in;

- Know that children can need protection, even in a family, and that they should tell someone if they need help;

- Realise that the *families* shown in adverts and the media are not the only model;

- Realise that there are organisations that help children and their parents so children are brought up healthy and can contribute to society.

Articles in the UN Convention on the Rights of the Child relevant to Unit 3:

- The right to be listened to (Article 12).

- The right to be cared for by 'parents' with support from the state (Article 18).

- The right to protection from abuse and neglect (Article 19).

- The right to protection if the family cannot provide it (Article 20).

- The right to protection from work that threatens the child's health, education or development (Article 32).

*It is important that a child feels **their family unit** and standard of living is acceptable and valued.*

*Many issues may be better tackled as hypotheses, rather than focusing on each child's own experience of **family**.*

The role of a family

Objective: For pupils to think about *families* as a unit that cares for and supports children.

Materials: Copies of **Once upon when** (page 62), **My family is special** (page 68).

Introduction

Discuss the meaning of a *family* so pupils embrace the concept of it being a very variable unit of people. Talk about what is nice about being in a *family*.

Activity 1

- List and discuss the roles played by each member of the *family*, e.g. mum can be a daughter, daughter-in-law, sister, auntie, cousin, niece, wife, granddaughter, stepmother, grandmother, etc.

- Pupils write a list of the relationship/role names which apply to them.

- Pupils list the relationship/roles for another *family* member.

Activity 2

- Pupils complete the writing frame **My family is special** on page 68, and list adjectives to describe each member of their family.

Activity 3

You can introduce your pupils to **Once upon when** in several ways: listen to the *Thursday's Child* CD or watch the video (see Resources page 127), read the words as if they were a poem, or learn the song.

- Pupils discuss the meaning of the song.

- In pairs, pupils circle key words in the song to do with having a family and a home.

- Pupils write a poem, or a song, expressing their feelings about living in a family. These can be shared at Circle time and children can offer supportive comments about each group's work.

Extension activities

- Pupils share their feelings about the song, suggest who might sing the song, and why.

- Pupils suggest the different ways children who find themselves in similar circumstances are helped.

Once upon when

In the half remembering mist of a dream,
Warm and soft like I've never known.
Once upon when
There's a memory of something beautiful,
Lost in a place I called home,
Once upon when I was young.

Once upon when there were voices
That rang with laughter,
Once, when I knew how to play.
Once upon then,
Is the memory that keeps my soul alive,
Knowing there's something called love,
Knowing that once I felt love.

I can still remember the scent of my Mother,
Father's arms held me safe and close.
Running to school,
I had friends, and peace, and play, and family,
Never knew hunger or fear,
Once, when my Mother was near.

Once upon when we made plans,
Then we had a future,
Once, when I knew how to hope,
Once upon then,
Is the memory that keeps my soul alive,
Knowing a place I called home,
Knowing that once I was home.

Once upon when
There's a memory of something beautiful,
Once, when I knew I was young.

Once Upon When

words and music by
Greg Snape

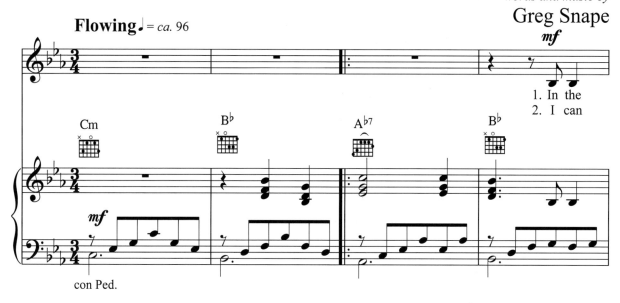

Flowing ♩ = ca. 96

con Ped.

1. In the
2. I can

half re - mem - ber-ing mist of a dream
still re - mem - ber the scent of my Mo - ther

Warm and soft like I've ne - ver known
Fa - ther's soft arms held me safe and close

Poco rit.

Once up-on when there's a me-mo-ry of some thing beau - ti - ful
Run - ning to school I had friends, and peace, and play, and fa - mi - ly

A♭7   B♭   Cm   B♭

A tempo

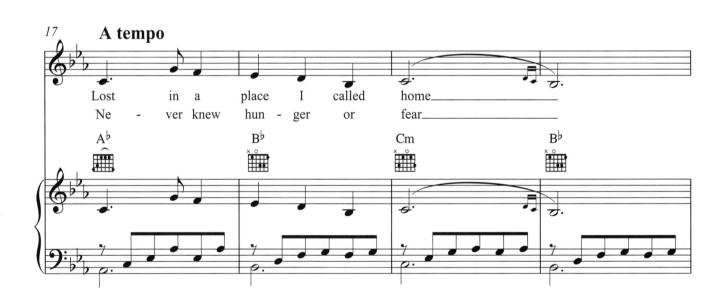

Lost in a place I called home_____
Ne - ver knew hun - ger or fear_____

A♭   B♭   Cm   B♭

Once up-on when I was young._____
Once, when my Mo - ther was near._____

A♭   B♭   Cm   B♭

Rit.

then   is   the   me - mo - ry   that   keeps   my   soul   a   live
then   is   the   me - mo - ry   that   keeps   my   soul   a - live

E♭   Fm   Gm⁶   G⁷sus⁴   G⁶

A tempo
mf

Know - ing there's   some - thing   called   love_____
Know - ing a   place   I   call   home_____

A♭   B♭   Cm   B♭

mf

Know - ing that   once   I   felt   love._____
Know - ing that   once   I   was   home._____

A♭   B♭   Cm   B♭

Once up-on when there's a me-mo-ry of some-thing

Rall. poco a poco

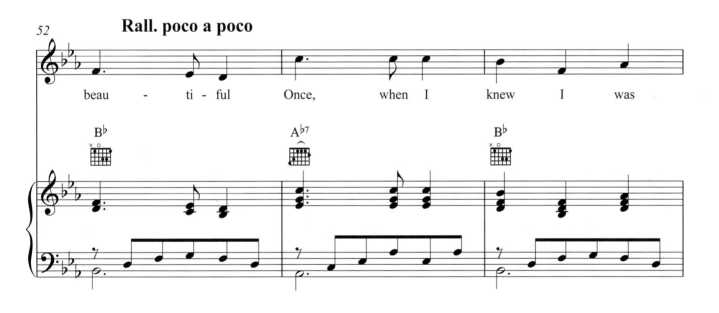

beau - ti - ful Once, when I knew I was

young.

My family is special

Name..Date..

Draw pictures of some of the members of your family in the boxes and complete the sentences.

My family is special because ....
....
....

I love my family because ....
....
....

love   share   care   laugh   comfort

soft   warm   fun   safe   peace

Care in the family

Objectives: For pupils to realise how family members care for each other.

Materials: Copies of **Saving a life** (page 73).

Introduction

List and discuss:

- **Which members of the family care for you? For example, mum, dad, brother, sister, grandparent, etc.**

- **In what ways are you cared for in the family? For example, right foods, a safe place to live, being loved, being given time, being clothed, having guide lines etc.**

- **Children too can be carers. How do all the people in a family care for each other?**

Activity

Saving a life

Pupils read the comic story **Saving a life**, which is taken from the Meena videos, produced for audiences in south-east Asia, see Resources page 127.

Plenary

Discuss:

- Who is caring in this family?

- How do people show their caring?

- Who else helps to care for baby Rani? (This also links with work on 'community'.)

- What might have happened if Rani's sister and brother hadn't found help?

- How might the story work out in this country?

- Can any pupils tell of a time when someone in their family 'saved a life'?

Circle time

Each pupil chooses one member of their 'family' and describes to the class how that person cares for them.

Extension activities

- Pupils draw members of their families who care for them, and write about how they care for them.

- Under the guise of 'caring', parents/family members sometimes make decisions about children that they do not like. What could they do about it?

One day, when Meena and Raju came home from school, they found that Meena's pet parrot Mithu has been locked in a cage by their aunt who is visiting them. But worse than this, mother says their baby sister Rani is ill.

Father is away from home, so Meena and Raju decide to go to their teacher for help. The wind is blowing hard and black storm clouds are gathering in the sky.

Meena and Raju bravely struggle through the storm and reach the house of their teacher. She is surprised to see them out in such bad weather.

Meanwhile, at home, a strong gust of wind has blown Mithu's cage down and he is able to escape. He follows Meena and flies through the storm to reach the teacher's house.

Carrying the important message, Mithu battles back through the storm to the house and tells mother and father, who has returned, what to do.

Why don't you give Rani some rice water. I'll go and find the children.

Imagine believing what a bird says!... No one listens to old people these days.

Just then, Meena and Raju come rushing through the door.

Did Mithu tell you what to do?

Yes, we've given Rani plenty to drink.

We must carry on giving her plenty to drink until the vomiting stops.

By next morning Rani is out of danger and gurgling happily in her cradle.

Later, their teacher visits the family to see if all is well. While she is there the teacher advises Meena's family about the baby's meals.

Family life

Objectives: For pupils to realise that there are differing family life styles and all have value. To recognise that the pictures of family life shown in advertisements are unrealistic and not typical.

Materials: Copies of **Meet the Family** (page 76), **The Family Tree** (page 77). The Extension activity requires copies of adverts, etc. showing families.

Introduction

You may have discussed what a family is and how all families are different in **The role of a family (page 61).**

Activity

- In pairs, pupils each receive a copy of **The Family Tree** (page 77). They look at it and discuss what information is given in it and the possible relationships between the people named.

- Then give pairs copies of the black and white picture of **Meet the Family**. They look at the picture and the family tree and discuss who is who. You may want to give them a few questions to help them start, e.g. Who is the youngest or oldest? Pupils write the people's names on the drawing. You might like them to colour the picture.

- Show the class the colour picture of **Meet the Family** (page 75). Pupils compare their own pictures with the colour picture which identifies the family members.

- Pupils draw a group portrait of their own family, and attempt a family tree.

Plenary

Pupils share their family portraits.

Extension activities

- Pupils collect adverts from magazines etc. that show 'families'.
- They compare them with the Family and their own families.
- Pupils list the similarities and differences between families in adverts and their own families.
- Pupils discuss what they have learnt about the way magazines depict families and their lifestyle?
- How do adverts make us feel about our own lives?
- Are advertisements a good or bad influence in our lives? Why? Why not?
- What attitude should we take towards advertisements?

Dilip

Anita Sanjay Meena

Suriya Vashi Raj Lakshmi

Ratna Danny John

Jenny

Katy Caroline

Fiona Shumin Ann

David Samantha
Billy
Keeley

Meet the Family

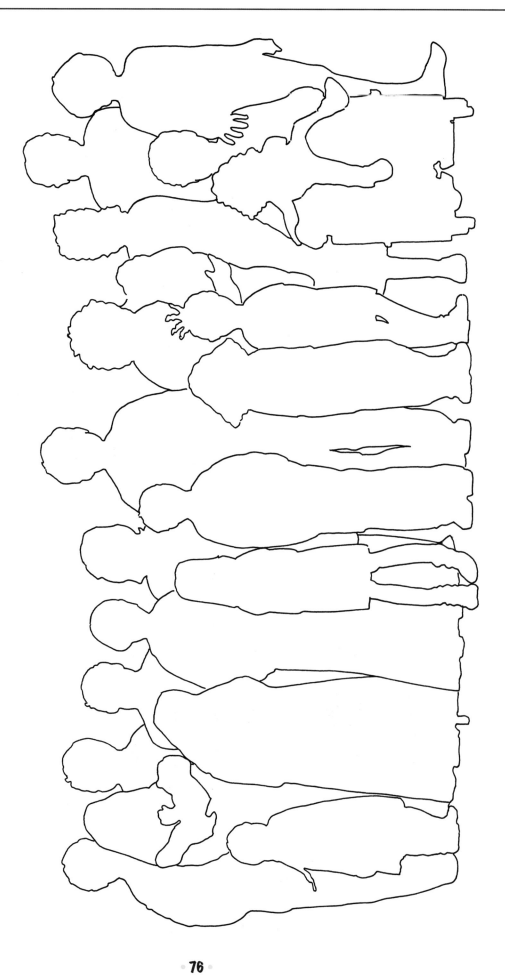

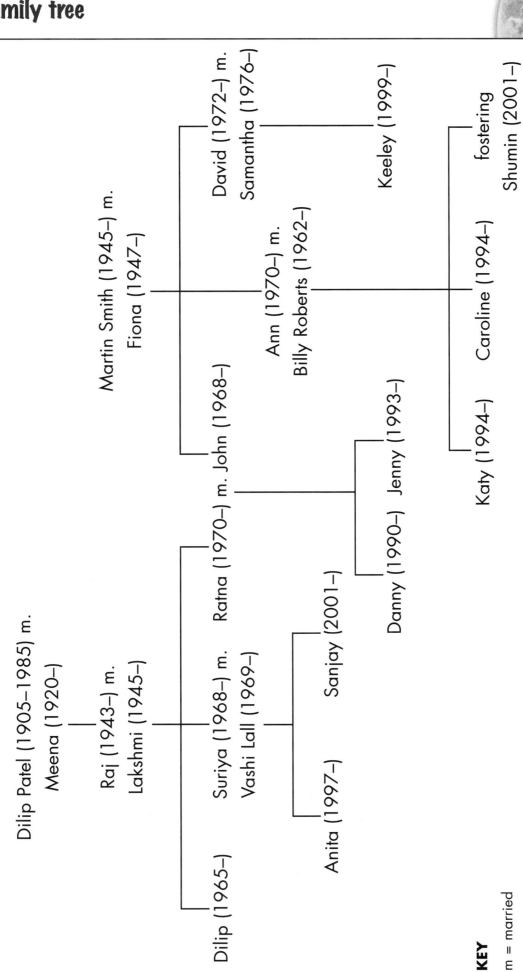

Dilip Patel (1905–1985) m.
Meena (1920–)

Raj (1943–) m.
Lakshmi (1945–)

Martin Smith (1945–) m.
Fiona (1947–)

Dilip (1965–)

Suriya (1968–) m.
Vashi Lall (1969–)

Ratna (1970–) m. John (1968–)

David (1972–) m.
Samantha (1976–)

Ann (1970–) m.
Billy Roberts (1962–)

Anita (1997–)

Sanjay (2001–)

Danny (1990–)

Jenny (1993–)

Katy (1994–)

Caroline (1994–)

Keeley (1999–)

fostering
Shumin (2001–)

KEY

m = married

(1943–) this means this person is still alive.

3.4 Children sometimes need protection

Objectives: For pupils to see that children all over the world are exploited and sometimes need protection, but that they are also often helping their families to survive.

Materials: Copies of **Helping the family** (page 79).

Introduction

Talk about children working (this links with the world family activity 3.6 (page 83) and how, in other countries, children often have to work long hours for little pay to help their families survive.

- **Read Helping the family.**
- **What is the work Lakshmi does?**
- **What is the main reason Lakshmi has to work?**
- **How is Lakshmi hurt by what she does?**
- **Should it be allowed?**

Activity

- In groups, pupils discuss what is good and bad about Lakshmi's life.
- What view do they take of: a) Lakshmi's parents? b) Lakshmi's employer?
- Should the employer have a responsibility towards Lakshmi? If so what should this be?
- What could be done to improve Lakshmi's life?
- Groups make a list of questions they would like to ask Lakshmi.
- The questions could be put to a pupil role-playing Lakshmi.

Extension activities

- Pupils find out what 'exploitation' means. Then decide if this applicable to Lakshmi's situation and give reasons for their opinion.
- This links with acitivity 5.4 Children's legal rights (page 115) where laws which apply to children in the UK are listed. Pupils could compare the kind of work they are allowed to do and when, with Lakshmi's work.

Helping the family – India

Lakshmi is about 10 years old. She works every day, seven days a week from 9 in the morning to 6 at night, making cigarettes. Lakshmi has to make 1,000 cigarettes a day to earn 200 rupees (£3.50) a month. She goes home for an hour to have a lunch of rice, dal, meat and pickle. She has been doing this every day for as long as she can remember.

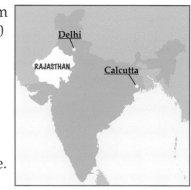

If you visit India you won't see girls like Lakshmi, because she does her work hidden from view in a dark smokey room in an ordinary family house. All day she sits cross-legged on the floor, part of a circle of six women and girls. First she rolls the tobacco leaves, then she stuffs them with loose tobacco.

Lakshmi's mother, and her younger sister Suraswati also make cigarettes. Her father has a cycle rickshaw but he doesn't earn much because he drinks. Lakshmi never plays, nor has she ever been to school, although she would like to go if her parents agreed. At home she has to help her mother by fetching water and sweeping the house.

The woman who employs Lakshmi has five children who all go to school. She said, "It's mostly those in debt who send their children to work for me. If they didn't send them I wouldn't take them. Lakshmi's parents live in a cycle of debt. They borrowed 2,000 rupees (£35.00) from me to pay off another debt, so Lakshmi has to work for me until she has paid it off."

This will probably never happen.

3.5 Tell someone

There are times when children need special support e.g. if they are abused, witness events they don't understand and find frightening, or face unexpected changes. This role-play activity provides an opportunity for children to discuss and explore difficult situations in an impersonal way and in a safe environment. It is important that a child understands it's all right to tell somebody about abnormal behaviour towards them and that they are not responsible for this behaviour.

Objectives: For pupils to learn that some types of behaviour by adults, siblings and peers is not acceptable.

Materials: Copies of **How Happiness told someone** (page 81) and copies of **Tell someone** role play cards (page 82).

The teacher needs to decide how to use the role-play cards from these options:

- All the groups use the same scenario;
- Give each scenario to two groups so there are opportunities to compare their responses;
- Each group has a different scenario;
- Will groups perform the scenarios to each other?

Introduction

Talk about how children need to be protected because they can't look after themselves – they are not big enough and they don't have enough money. But unfortunately, although most adults are caring, sometimes they are not and children need to know what to do if something bad happens.

Read How Happiness told someone and discuss how she managed to improve her life.

Activity

- Give small groups of pupils one of the **Tell someone** role-play cards to dramatise and prepare to show.
- Pupils join forces with another group, maybe a group with the same role-play, perform their plays for each other and discuss the best solution;
- Or: groups show their role-plays to the class in turn and the class discuss the solutions.
- In each case pupils decide the best solution to the situation.

Plenary

- Discuss the solutions pupils found to the role-plays.
- Discuss and list the different people children might turn to for help, and what to do if that person doesn't listen.
- Provide information about the organisations children can turn to for help.

How Happiness told someone - Tanzania

Happiness is 12 years old but her life has not been very happy so far. This is how she tells her story.

"A year ago I went to live with my mother's cousin who promised that he would look after me in his house and send me to school. But he didn't send me to school at all. Instead I had to babysit his three-year-old baby all the time. His wife beat me a lot for no reason at all. Whenever she beat me she would tell her husband that I had done something wrong, then he would beat me too with a stick or a big wooden cooking spoon. In the summer, when there was a water shortage, they made me walk two hours to the well to fetch water and then two hours back.

"One day I felt sick so I told them I couldn't get water. She beat me really hard that day so I escaped to a house in town where a friendly grandfather took me in. But that night my mother's cousin turned up and took me back to his house. He beat me so badly that stuff was coming out of my ears. I went to the hospital and they told me I have malaria and my ear is also bad.

"Fortunately another relative brought me to Dar es Salaam and got me a job as a domestic worker with another relative who is kind to me. I get paid a little each month and I go to the Kiwohedo Drop-in Centre where I am learning to read and write. My hearing is permanently damaged and I need an operation to repair my left ear."

When asked what she wished for her future Happiness replied, "Education, and a second-hand dress."

1. Jack is five years old. He has a brother, Tom, who is 10 years old. Jack and Tom spend a lot of time alone together, but Jack is frightened of Tom.

When they are alone together, Tom breaks up Jack's games with his toy cars and has 'mock-fights' with him. But Tom is a lot bigger and heavier and takes no notice when Jack screams. Jack always has bruises on his arms and legs.

Jack decided to tell his father. What happens when he does?

2. Lisa is seven years old. Several nights a week she is looked after by Marie who is a lot older than her. Sometimes Marie is kind and plays with Lisa, but when her boyfriend, John, comes round, Marie is quite nasty to Lisa.

She makes Lisa go in her bedroom even when it's not bedtime. If Lisa comes out Marie or John shout at her, and once John hit her quite hard.

Lisa told her aunt Hazel. What happens when Hazel tells Lisa's mother?

3. Tracey's mum, Kim, has a brother called Jason. Jason often comes round to see Kim and he always brings sweets for Tracey. At first Tracey liked Jason but one day he took her to the cinema and he kept stroking her legs.

Kim thinks it's nice that her brother likes Tracey and now Kim has to go into hospital and says she is going to leave Jason to look after Tracey for a night or two. But Tracey is frightened that Jason might try to touch her again.

Tracey tells her best friend, Jo, who tells her mother, Betsy. Betsy decides to talk to Kim. What happens when she does?

4. Dawn and Tony's mother is not well. She finds it hard to keep the house clean and do the shopping. Often Dawn and Tony don't get any proper meals at home except what they can find for themselves in the cupboard. Sometimes Dawn steals money from her mother's purse and buys chips for herself and Tony.

Once their mother was put in a hospital and they were put in a home. They hated it and don't want that to happen again.

Dawn and Tony decide to tell Dawn's teacher. What happens when they do?

The world family

This section suggests ways children can share what they have learnt about themselves and the way all families are different but all valued, and that sometimes children need protection.

- If you haven't already done so do the activity **A Place in the world for me** (page 57), where pupils show where they have family and friends on a world map and display this. Pupils can share this in an assembly or with a display.

- Pupils prepare and perform a number of scenes which show the different caring relationships within a family.

- Pupils learn and perform the song **Once upon when** (pages 63-67). This could be linked with Lakshmi's story (page 79) and a performance about children's need for care and protection, worldwide, and how they look to adults to provide it. Another appropriate song is **The family of man**.

Research

Pupils write to or read about organisations which exist to help children.

Globalisation

Read this story which shows the effects of the global economy in Thailand, to your pupils.

Jom, aged 14, is working somewhere in Bangkok because a financial crisis has plunged her family into deep poverty. It started when Jom's brother Boonthun wanted to buy a motorbike to start a taxi business. Her mother put up their land as security. The interest on the loan was a colossal 60%, but Mrs Sa Ud wasn't worried as she had three other children sending money home from their jobs in Bangkok. However, when the financial crisis hit Thailand, hundreds of thousands of people lost their jobs as companies folded – including Mrs Sa Ud's three children. Boonthun had trouble keeping up the payments on the motorbike and the interest rate soared. Mrs Sa Ud took out another loan to pay the first. She sold the family home and all their valuable goods: the motorbike, cooking pots, electric fan. They rented out their farmland. The other three children came home from Bangkok and needed supporting. Jom, who already had a higher level of education than any of her brothers and sisters, had to leave school and look for work. She went to Bangkok, a dangerous city for girls from the countryside. The family hasn't heard from her since.

Homework

- Pupils could research the effects of globalisation on families. Ask them to look for news reports, etc. about how changes in the world economy can affect families, a) in the UK; b) in other countries where there is no social security to support them.

- Pupils engage their families in helping them to draw up a family tree.

What do rights mean in school?

Activities which examine the purpose of school and education and ways of increasing pupil participation; also respecting difference, establishing an agreed moral code and standing up to peer pressure.

Activities will help your pupils:

- Explore the purpose of their education;
- Recognise that everyone in the school has rights;
- Look at their school and how they can participate within it;
- Recognise that in any community each person is a unique individual and should be valued as such;
- Realise that by taking responsibility for themselves they make a difference to each other's lives;
- Know that by their actions they can change the lives of people they meet every day;
- Develop skills of self-confidence, be able to express a view point, listen to others and withstand peer pressure if necessary.

Articles in the UN Convention on the Rights of the Child relevant to Unit 4:

- All children have all rights (Article 2).
- The right to express an opinion and be listened to (Article 12).
- The right to information (Article 13).
- The purpose of education (Article 29).
- School discipline should be consistent with the child's human dignity (Article 28).

The purpose of education

Objective: For pupils to think about the purpose of their education.

Materials: Copies of **Education for Life the Yanomami way** (page 86) and **The purpose of education** (page 87), illustrations and statements for pupils to share.

Introduction

List and discuss the reasons your pupils give for being at school.

Tell them that in countries in Africa, Asia and Latin America, 130 million children do not go to school and most of them wish they could. You could refer back to Lakshmi, 3.4 (page 79), she would love the chance to go to school.

Also discuss that if every child has the right to an education, a child that disrupts lessons is depriving others in the class of this right.

Activity 1

- Pupils match the five statements with the five illustrations on page 87.

- In addition, make up one statement and illustrate it.

- Pupils share their additional purpose of education.

Activity 2

- Read the description of Kiko's education on page 86.

- Which of the five purposes of education does his education fit?

Plenary

Discuss:

- Does every child need exactly the same education?

- What aspects of their education do your pupils think the most and least important?

Extension activities

- Pupils write about the things that they would like to see changed in the school. This can be a preparation for 4.2 **Who is in our school and what rights do they need?** (page 88).

Kiko is a Yanomami Indian, one of the largest groups of forest peoples in South America who still live traditionally. His home is the Amazon rainforest.

He lives with his family and several other families in a large, roughly circular house, called a *maloca*. Each family has its own fire and cooking area and space to hang their hammocks, but each family's area opens into the central meeting area, which has a hole in the roof to let the smoke out. Now a propped-up blackboard shows where there is a new section in Kiko's *maloca* – an area for school.

For Yanomami children education is what they need to learn to survive, and they learn it from everyone in their village. But even though the Yanomami want to preserve their traditional way of life, they see advantages in learning to read and write both their own language and Portuguese.

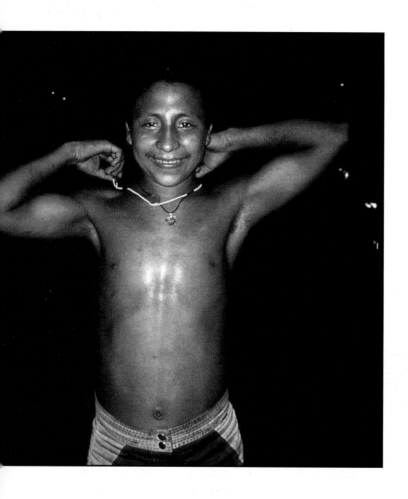

Most days Kiko gets up early and goes fishing with a line and hook in the nearby river. He also likes to hunt turtles, monkeys and a kind of boar, as well as birds – parrots and blackbirds. Sometimes he collects fruit from the nearby clearing in the forest where the families grow corn, sweet potato and cassava, banana and plantain trees. In the photograph, Kiko is showing us the jewelry he has made out of beads and string. Fishing, hunting, what to eat and where to find it, and craftwork - all these skills he learned from his people. But now, in the afternoon he has language classes with the other children, and anyone who wishes to join in. He likes school and understands more Portuguese than he speaks.

Kiko is about 14 years old and soon he may be married. Then he will be responsible for his wife's parents so he needs to be a good provider. His wife will be taught all she needs to know about housekeeping, cooking and childcare by her mother. But since his wife is quite likely to be a girl he has grown up with in the village, he will never be far from those who can advise and help him.

The purpose of education

Education should develop the child's personality and talents to their fullest potential.	Education should develop respect for human rights and fundamental freedoms.	The development of respect for cultural identities - both your own and other people's.

Children should develop respect for the natural environment.	Preparation for life in a free society, with tolerance and equality and friendship among all peoples.

4.2 Who is in our school and what rights do they need?

Objective: For pupils to realise that school is a place for education with a specialist body of learners and teachers, and all these people have rights.

Materials: Copies of **Work and rights** (page 89).

Introduction

Hold a thought-shower about the people who make up the school community.

(So far work has concentrated on children's rights, but everyone has similar rights, adults too – under the Human Rights Act of 2000 and the Universal Declaration of Human Rights.)

Activity

Working in **pairs** pupils select one or more of the people from the thought shower list, **write** a brief description of their role within the school and think of one right that particular person would like to have respected, e.g. to be spoken to respectfully, for everyone to say 'please' and 'thank you', etc. Pupils can draw a portrait of the appropriate person in each box.

Plenary

- The class share their work then complete the sheet **Work and rights**.

- School 'staff' could be invited to visit the classroom to talk about their role with your pupils and to see what right they would say they would particularly like respected.

- Or your pupils could write a letter to all adults in the schools, asking them what right they would particularly like respected (this might pose problems if other adults in the school are not conversant with the language and content of rights). If adults visit the classroom then there can be a dialogue and it can be a way of introducing them to rights.

Work and rights

Write two sentences about these people in school:

Sentence one, about the work they do.

Sentence two, about one right that they might need to have respected.

Draw pictures of these people doing their work.

School secretary	Teacher	Classroom assistant
Caretaker	Kitchen staff	Pupils

Who would you most like to help, and why?

I would like to help the .... with their work because..

....

4.3 My school today

Objective: To help pupils express their opinions and impressions about their school, and for them to be listened to.

Materials: Copies of **My School today** (page 91), scissors, adhesive, paper.

Two different activities are suggested for this sheet. Half the class could do Activity 1: True/false activity, and the other half Activity 2: Ranking activity.

Introduction

- Talk about how you, the teacher, felt about going to school, then ask your pupils how they feel about school.

- Tell them that nowadays pupils are more likely to be listened to and their views on their school taken into consideration. The following activity/s will help them think about school constructively.

- Pupils discuss "School is a great place to come to each day".

Activity 1

- Pupils working in pairs first read, then cut up the statements on **My school today.** They should add their own statements too.

- Pupils decide which ones they think are true and which are untrue and they place them in two columns headed 'True' and 'Untrue'.

(If you want your pupils to go on and do Activity 2, then tell them not to stick them down, unless you are going to give them another copy.)

Activity 2

- Pupils working in pairs/groups rank the cut-up statements from **My school today** in order of importance, i.e. the one they think is the most important is number 1 (pupils should ignore the numbers on the statements, these are for easy reference).

- Pupils stick their statements onto a piece of paper for display.

Plenary

- Pupils display their work.

- Pupils are given the opportunity to comment on and ask questions about the work.

Extension activity

Pupils write about their school:

- Its good and bad points;

- How they would like to see the school change.

My school today

1. Pupils are shown how to be responsible for their own studying.

2. Teachers listen to pupils' opinions on matters that concern them.

3. Pupils are consulted about the clothes they wear in school.

4. School is a safe place for all pupils.

5. There is no bullying in the school.

6. All pupils are treated equally.

7. All pupils respect their teachers.

8. All teachers respect their pupils.

9. Pupils like playtime.

10. Pupils make decisions with their teachers about how the classroom is run.

11. All pupils are happy in school.

12.

4.4 School rules

Objectives: For pupils to understand how and why school rules are made and to contribute their own ideas.

Materials: whiteboard, copy of the school rules for reference.

Introduction

Explain to your pupils that they are going to look at and think about the rules within the school.

Activity

Read and discuss the school rules and the class rules, in the order you think most appropriate.

In groups, pupils discuss and prepare an answer to questions such as:

- Which rules would they change? Why would they like to change them?
- Which rules they would like to make? Why would they like to make them?
- Do pupils have a voice in the making of school rules?
- Do pupils have a voice in the making of class rules?
- Each group reports their findings.

Plenary

The class shares and discusses the answers and decides what action, if any, is needed.

Extension activity

Article 28 of the Convention states "that school discipline is administered in a manner consistent with the child's human dignity."

- Discuss the discipline administered in the school and whether or not it undermines pupils sense of dignity.

School councils

Objectives: For pupils to hear and think about pupils' participation in school in another country, and compare it to their own experience.

Materials: Copies of **Elections at Calle Larga New School** (page 94), and a world map.

Introduction

- **Find Colombia on a world map.**

- **Explore the pupils' perceptions and knowledge of Colombia. This is particularly pertinent if you have used the previous Colombia Case Study, Children using their rights (page 43).**

Activity

- Read **Elections at Calle Larga New School**.

- List and discuss the responsibilities that the student councillors have at Calle Larga New School.

- List and discuss those that the student councillors have at your school and compare them.

Plenary

Pupils compare and contrast their experience of participation in school with the experience described in Calle Larga New School.

If your school does not have a school council, or it needs reforming, then this could be a topic for the class. Schools Councils UK is an organisation which helps schools with councils and Save the Children has a resource 'The School Council – a Children's Guide. Addresses in the Resources section (page 126-7).

An official spokesperson for the students stated:

"It was a hard fought election and the results are expected to be close." She added: *"The new members of the council will be overseeing all student activities, including the running of the school garden, daily school maintenance and giving their opinion on the day to day running of the school."*

Estola, aged nine years, and Maria Adelie, aged eight, are monitors at the elections for student councillors which takes place at their school, Calle Larga New School, close to the city of Amenia in Colombia. Another student casts her vote for the person she thinks would best represent the students on the Student Council. In Colombia, student councils are commonly held as part of Education for Citizenship and new student councils are elected several times a year to oversee all student activities.

In the weeks leading up to the elections there is election fever, and the four candidates nominated to fill two positions on the School Council each led a fierce campaign to try to get themselves elected.

The results of the election are posted in the school later in the day when all students have voted.

My school tomorrow

Objective: For pupils to express their opinions on how they would like their school to be.

Materials: Copies of **My school tomorrow** (page 96), scissors, adhesive, paper.

Introduction

List and discuss the features pupils would like to see in school.

Activity

Pupils working in pairs/groups read and complete My school tomorrow.

Plenary

- Pupils display their work.
- Pupils are given the opportunity to comment on or question the work presented.

My school tomorrow

Read these suggestions from a group of 11 year-old children. In the blank squares add any ideas of your own.

Cut the suggestions out and decide which 10 items you consider the most important. Stick the ideas onto a piece of paper with the most important one at the top.

1. Laptops for every teacher and pupil	**2.** Pupils help in the selection of new staff	**3.** C.C.T.V. (surveillance cameras)
4. Air conditioning	**5.** Designer toilets	**6.** Pupil governors
7. An 'on site' school counsellor for pupils	**8.** Pupils have a say in the decoration of the school	**9.** Recreation rooms with fitness equipment
10. A safe route to walk or cycle to school	**11.** Single sex classes	**12.** Flexible school hours
13. Automatic access for all pupils to email children across the world	**14.** Video links - for 'home learning' between school and pupils' homes	**15.** All pupils have a say and decide the school rules
16. Pupils have a say in what they are taught.	**17.** Pupils have a high level of responsibility for themselves and each other	**18.**
19.	**20.**	**21.**

Who's in your group?

Objective: For pupils to see that they have things in common with many of their peers, including those who they may think of as being very different from themselves in terms of gender, race, ethnicity and social class.

Materials: Space in which pupils can move freely and make some noise.

Introduction

Talk about how we all see ourselves as being members of certain groups. This activity will help them see that they have things in common with many members of the class.

Warning: avoid using characteristics that will cause pupils to group themselves along lines of ethnicity, race, class or appearance, etc. if this may prove divisive.

Activity

Call out a series of characteristics, one at a time. After you call each one, pupils move around the room to form small groups with others who have the same characteristic. For example, if the characteristic is 'favourite colour', pupils walk round quietly saying their favourite colour. When two students with the same favourite colour find each other, they then move around together looking for others with the same response until small groups sharing the same response are formed. Pupils spend a few minutes in this group discussing the characteristic they have in common, and then separate to group themselves according to the next characteristic you call out.

Characteristics that might be used are:

- Favourite food, lesson, pop group, TV show, etc.
- How many brothers/sisters pupils have.
- What time pupils get up, etc.

Plenary

In groups/class discuss:

- Did you find yourself in a group with someone you didn't expect to have anything in common with? Why was this a surprise?
- What new things did you learn about your classmates?
- Which group did you enjoying being in most of all? Why was this?
- Was there a different feeling being in a big or small group? Why? Why not?
- How did it feel if you were in a very small group, or even alone? How did this make you feel about the bigger groups?
- Are there any lessons we can learn about the way we interact with other pupils in the school? Or in things we do outside school?

4.8 It's OK to be different

Objectives: For pupils to get a new perspective on 'being different', and to see that being different can be very positive.

Materials: The boy with two eyes page 99.

Introduction

● **Read the story to the class.**

● **Discuss it briefly so everyone understands what it is about.**

Activity

● Working in groups pupils, list the advantages and disadvantages of being the 'boy with two eyes'.

● Children present their group work.

● As a class, make a comprehensive list of the advantages and disadvantages of being the 'boy with two eyes'.

Plenary

● Pupils discuss if, in the end, it mattered that the boy with two eyes was different?

● Why do some people treat people with a disability differently?

● Are disabled children excluded from groups? If so, does the type/level of disability alter the groups they are excluded from, and why?

Extension activities

● Discuss how people with a disability feel about themselves and the way people treat them.

● Pupils talk or write about the disability they consider the most difficult to live with, and why they feel this.

List and discuss the fact that people are differently 'abled'. For example, children with outstanding ability in sport, maths, drama, or people at the other end of the scale, can all be singled out for special attention that makes them different from their peers.

● Each child says what their positive unique difference is. (See activities 2.1 and 2.3 - **I am special** and **Helping others feel good** - pages 47 and 51.)

● Each child then says what their neighbour's positive unique difference is.

The boy with two eyes

Way, way out in space, there is a planet just like Earth. The people who live on the planet are just like us, except for one thing, they have only one eye. But it is a very special eye. With their one eye they can see in the dark. They can see far, far away; and they can see straight through walls.

Women on this planet have children, just like on Earth.

One day a strange child was born. He had two eyes! His mother and father were very upset.

The boy was a happy child. His parents loved him and enjoyed looking after him, but they were worried because he was so unusual. They took him to lots of doctors. The doctors shook their heads and said, "Nothing can be done."

As the child grew up, he had more and more problems. Since he couldn't see in the dark, he had to carry a light. When he went to school, he could not read as well as other children. His teachers had to give him extra help. He couldn't see long distances, so he had to have a special telescope. Then he could see the stars and other planets. Sometimes when he walked home from school he felt very lonely. "Other children see things I can't see," he thought. "I must be able to see things they don't see."

And one exciting day, he discovered he could see something that nobody else could see. He did not see in black and white as everybody else did. He told his parents how he saw things. He took his parents outside and told them about his thrilling discovery. They were amazed! His friends were amazed as well. He told them wonderful stories. He used words they had never heard before... like red... and yellow... and orange. He talked about green trees and purple flowers. Everybody wanted to know how he saw things. He told wonderful stories about deep blue seas and waves with foaming white tops. Children loved to hear his stories about amazing dragons. They gasped as he described their skin, their eyes and their fiery breath.

One day he met a girl. They fell in love and got married. She didn't mind that he had two eyes. And then he found that he didn't mind either. He had now become very famous. People came from all over the planet to hear him talk.

Eventually they had a son. The child was just like all the other children on the planet. He had only one eye.

What's acceptable behaviour?

Objective: For pupils to discuss and decide what behaviour is acceptable and what is unacceptable.

Materials: Each group needs copies of **What's acceptable** (pages 101-102) (preferably pre-cut), blank cards, adhesive, a sheet of A3 paper with the following headings:

Acceptable behaviour	Not sure	Unacceptable behaviour

Care may be needed about the composition and size of the groups.

Introduction

Remind your pupils how appropriate behaviour was discussed as part of Unit 2, activity 3 (page 51). This activity looks at pupils' behaviour more broadly and asks them to decide what they think is acceptable, and what is not.

Activity

- Arrange pupils in groups of up to eight. Select a facilitator for each group to run the discussion. Give each facilitator a copy of the statements, the A3 sheet of paper with three headings and some adhesive. The facilitator keeps the cards in front of him or her, letting each member of the group draw from it in turn. Throughout, the facilitator manages the discussion and ensures that only one person speaks at once and that everyone has an opportunity to speak.

- In turn, each member of the group draws a card. They read it to the group and then decide in which column to place it, explaining to the others why they made that decision.

- This is then open to discussion. If people disagree, they can try to persuade the person to move the card to another column. The pupil listens to the views and has the right to move the card to another column or leave it where it is.

- The card is then stuck in place.

- The pupils continue the activity until all the cards have been read and stuck to the sheet.

- Display and discuss the results.

Plenary

Discuss who decides on what is 'acceptable' and 'unacceptable behaviour' in school.

Extension activity

In groups, pupils review the "Unacceptable behaviour" cards, and list ways how these situations could be stopped in school.

What's acceptable?

To call people by racist names.	To be told a secret and to tell it to someone else.
To call disabled people names.	To write graffiti on a wall.
To tease or taunt another person by calling them names that are unkind.	To leave things in a mess for someone else to tidy up.
For boys or girls to say nice things about each other.	To help someone with their work.
To be nasty about a friend or ex-friend.	To be courteous and polite to others.
To bully someone, either by physically hitting or verbally abusing them.	To "tell" on somebody to a teacher or concerned adult.
To make rude remarks about anyone's physical appearance.	To steal from a friend or classmate.
To try always to do your best work.	To say "No" when you are asked to be part of a wrongdoing.

What's acceptable?

To understand and learn to say 'No' to drugs.

To be interested in your schoolwork.

To judge someone by what they are wearing.

To do homework and study.

To say 'No' to an adult when asked to do something that you shouldn't or that scares you.

To encourage angry people to fight.

To write graffiti.

To be punished for lying or cheating.

To disobey a teacher.

To drop litter.

To be rude to a teacher.

To smash public property like desks or classroom equipment

To praise someone who has done well.

To stand by your friend when everyone else is slagging him or her off.

My rights, your rights

Objectives: To develop pupils' understanding that the rights they hold are also held by every child and adult.

To develop the skills, and the self-confidence, necessary to confront and stand up to bullying, peer pressure and prejudice.

Materials: Copies of **My rights, your rights** situation cards (page 104), and dictionaries.

Introduction

Pupils refer to the definition of 'rights' decided upon at the beginning of this work, or look it up in the dictionary. Explain that this is a role-play activity when they should take the situation described on their card and work out what they should do.

Activity

- Divide the class into groups of four and give each group a **My rights, your rights** situation card.

- Everyone in the group reads their **My rights, your rights** situation card.

- They decide who will act out the situation and who will be the observers.

- The scene is acted out and the group discusses the scene. The observers give feedback about which approach they thought would work best in challenging the prejudice which was expressed.

- Groups amend the scene in light of the discussion and act it out again, this time with the observers as the actors.

- The group may then want to discuss and amend the play even further.

- Each group performs their play. One pair present their play and the other couple briefly explain their group discussions.

Plenary

Pupils share what they have learned from this activity.

Extension activities

- Pupils discuss how the role play situations were similar and how they were different

- Pupils express how it felt to play the part of the biased person.

- Pupils explain how it felt to play the part of the person who challenged the prejudice.

1. Your class teacher is ill and your class has had several supply teachers. Some children behave so badly that the teachers haven't stayed. Now you have a teacher who is giving the class interesting but quite difficult work.

Some of the class are playing up again but you like the teacher and want to do the work. When your friend says,

"What are you doing that for? She's only a supply teacher."

You respond, "...

2. It is Sonia's first day in your class. Sonia uses a wheelchair to move around. One of your friends says to you,

"I'm going to help Sonia with this comprehension exercise because she probably won't be able to do it on her own."

You say, "...

3. You are a girl who has recently fallen out with your best friend, Fiona. Marie is trying to be your best friend. One day she says to you,

"Look at Fiona's jacket! Where did she get it? She really looks a mess!"

You say, "...

4. Jena is a girl who has recently joined your class from another country. One day you are eating lunch when one of your friends says to you,

"Look at that weird food that Jena brought for lunch! Doesn't it smell disgusting? How can she eat that stuff? Don't they eat normal food in her country?"

You answer, "...

This section suggests ways children can actively share what they have learned about themselves and their school, and what they have learned about respecting others' right to respect. Also to stand up to those who threaten other people's rights by words or actions.

- The work on their school and the people in it can be presented to the whole school.

- The class could undertake a review of the school council, devising ways to assess its effectiveness and whether pupils are happy with the way it operates. Do pupils really have "a voice" in decisions that affect them and their fellow pupils. Are requests listened to, considered and responded to?

- The role play activities in 'My rights, your rights' (page 104) could be presented in assembly, similarly 'The Boy with Two Eyes' (page 99) could be dramatised for assembly.

Research

For more information about running a School or Classroom Council, contact Schools Councils UK (see Resources page 127).

Homework

Pupils could ask parents or grandparents:

- What rules did their schools have and how were they expected to behave?

- What was the relationship like between teachers and pupils?

- What did they enjoy about school and wished they could have done more of? What didn't they like about school?

- How were they punished?

- What did they learn in school that has been of use to them in their lives?

- Did they have school councils?

- Also, were they ever bullied? If so, what did they do?

What do rights mean in the community?

Activities to help children realise their right to participate fully in community life and to be heard on issues important to them.

Activities will help your pupils:

- Understand that they are part of a community and they can make a positive or negative difference to their own and other people's lives;
- Know that by their actions they can change the lives of people they meet every day;
- Believe that by taking responsibility for themselves they make a difference to each other's lives;
- Understand that they have legal rights and civil rights, and can exercise these;
- Practise the skills which will help them become participating citizens, making their voices and views known;
- Develop skills of self-confidence and self-expression, and working together.

Articles in the UN Convention on the Rights of the Child relevant to Unit 5:

- Children as rights bearers (Articles 1 and 2).
- Children's right to be heard (Article 12).
- Children's right to information (Article 13).
- Children's right to meet together (Article 15).

What is a community and do I have a part to play?

Objective: For pupils to understand the area of their own community and to use the stories from India to show how children in other parts of the world are involved in helping children in their community.

Materials: Large map or individual map/s of the area. Copies of **Children with a voice in the community** (page 108) and **Children playing a part in the community** (page 109).

Introduction

- **Display a map of your area and mark the community boundaries.**
- **Pupils to identify places of importance where they live e.g. faith centres, community centres, schools, doctors, dentist, council, etc.**

Using the case studies

Read **Children with a voice in the community** (page 108).

- Discuss what Dikan and the children do at the 'Bal Panchayat'.
- Do any of your pupils have a voice like this on their local council? (In the UK many councils also have initiatives like this.)

Read **Children playing a part in the community** (page 109).

- Discuss the two community initiatives Kalamuddin is involved in.
- Are any of your class involved in similar projects?

Activity

- Groups make a list of questions they would like to ask Dikan and Kalamuddin.
- Pupils contact the local council and ask about the representation of young people on the local council. Is there a way they can make their voice heard? Can one of them be on the youth council?
- Groups decide on a short list of things would like to see changed in the community.

Extension activities

- Discuss the case study with the idea of the class developing an issue the class feel strongly about. It could be an issue that would make a difference to the community.
- Develop an action plan and implement it. See activity 5.5 (pages 117-121), **Running a campaign.**

Bal = children   Panchayat = administrative council of a village.

Dikan Chand, in the patterned shirt, is 12 years old and the Deputy Head of the Bal Panchayat of a village in the state of Rajasthan. On his right is the Head, 15 year-old Saroche. The Bal Panchayat consists of nine children, five boys and four girls, they are all at secondary school. Each one has been elected by other children to represent their 'ward' or section of the village.

The Bal Panchayat meets once a month and all the village children can come to express their views on how to improve life in the village. The Bal Panchayat then take these views to the village council meeting.

Dikan thinks the most successful thing they have done is to help with the polio vaccination days. The Bal Panchayat went from house to house checking that all the children had been vaccinated.

So far the children have asked that the village schools should have better toilets and a supply of clean drinking water, and proper playgrounds for the schools. They would also like a bus service to outlying villages so children of all ages can come to the village schools, and they would like streetlights. The village council has taken action on some of these, but for some they say there is no money.

Dikan says,

"I have responsibilities towards other children. We are working for their education, trying to persuade their parents to let them go to school, and for schools to be better. And if there is a quarrel between children we try to solve it."

Kalamuddin, aged 12, lives in one of the poorest districts of the Indian city of Calcutta, an area that is famous and feared for its crime, drugs and violence. Kalamuddin is taking part in a project that helps children develop drama skills to write and act out plays about issues that the group is concerned about. Issues like, drugs, alcohol abuse, HIV/AIDS and discrimination against girls.

They perform the plays in the community to people of all ages. The plays help to start discussions between young people and adults, and encourage them to think of possible solutions to the most urgent problems in their community.

Kalamuddin also belongs to a children's club that gives children the chance to get together and play and forget their worries in a safe environment. The members of the club also reach out to other children who have come to Calcutta to work and who have family support in the city. Kalamuddin described some of these children:

"I know several children who've come to the city to work. They work in the hotels cooking food, and making breakfast. We in the club tell them that there's something more to life than just working – like education and playing. So sometimes on Saturdays we get these children to come to this place so that they can play here and have a good time. When they come here they feel happy because they can play games and they can get involved with us. Otherwise they don't get the chance to do these things. We have no problems with caste or religion, because whatever people are, they are our friends and we all stick together. Everyone is welcome and has a free say."

Living together in the community

Objective: For pupils to understand that both attitudes and behaviour can affect the way they are viewed in the community.

Materials: Copies of **A moral tale** (page 111) and **People in the moral tale** (page 112).

Activity

Read **A moral tale** to the class.

Discuss the message of the story. If necessary pose these questions:

- Why was the first woman turned away from the town?
- Why was the second woman allowed in?
- What was the gatekeeper trying to find out about the visitors who came to the town?
- What type of community did the people in the town want?

In pairs, pupils discuss and complete **People in the moral tale**. The point is, of course, that while the people in the town may have been a mixture of pleasant and unpleasant, how you are treated often depends on your own attitude toward others.

Plenary

List and discuss the adjectives they selected in the activity.

- Can any of the pupils think of an incident, similar to that in the story, that has happened to them or one of their family?

Extension

- Pupils write a description of a person using at least five adjectives from the class list.
- Pupils working in groups make up a poem 'People in our community', using as many adjectives from the class list as possible.
- Discuss the saying, "Sticks and stones may break my bones but words can never hurt me." Is this really true?
- How do words used about us, both negative and positive, affect our behaviour and the way we feel about ourselves?
- Write a paragraph about how recipients of negative words/verbal abuse may feel?

Circle time

- Each pupil turns to the person next to them and says a positive phrase about them.
- Each child offers a phrase they would like people to use to describe them.

A moral tale

A woman went to live in a new town, and as she came to the gate, the gatekeeper asked her,

"What were the people like in the town you have travelled from?"

She replied,

"They were bad tempered, quarrelsome, gossiping and generally unpleasant."

The gatekeeper then said,

"You will find the people here just as bad so I suggest you go on your way."

A second woman came along, and the gatekeeper asked her the same question, to which she replied,

"The people in the town I have travelled from were kind and caring. They were brave in times of trouble and they were always willing to share with me and to welcome strangers."

The gatekeeper then said,

"Come in, for you will find the people here just as welcoming and helpful."

People in the moral tale

Name...Date...

Draw a picture of the first woman who **wasn't** allowed into the town, and write down six adjectives to describe her.

```
┌─────────────────────────────────────────┐
│                                         │
│                                         │
│                                         │
│                                         │
│                                         │
│                                         │
│                                         │
│                                         │
│                                         │
└─────────────────────────────────────────┘
```

....

....

Draw a picture of the first woman who was allowed into the town, and write down six adjectives to describe her.

```
┌─────────────────────────────────────────┐
│                                         │
│                                         │
│                                         │
│                                         │
│                                         │
│                                         │
│                                         │
│                                         │
│                                         │
└─────────────────────────────────────────┘
```

....

....

Being a good citizen

Objectives: Pupils look at an example of what being a 'good' citizen means.

Materials: Copies of **Hidden hero** (page 114)

Introduction

- **Read Hidden hero with the class.**

- **Give copies of the story and its questions to pairs or groups of pupils.**

Activity

- Working in groups, pupils discuss the article and answer the questions.

- Pupils look at the questions they cannot answer positively, e.g. whether they know any first aid, and decide on a short list of things they need to find out.

Plenary

- Children present their findings.

- Decide on an action plan which will help equip your pupils to deal with a situation like this.

Extension activities

Article 28 of the Convention states "that school discipline is administered in a manner consistent with the child's human dignity."

- You, or pupils, could make up other situations like this which test their knowledge and reactions as to what to do in an emergency in the community.

- In an average year, over 50% of 999 calls are hoaxes. Talk about the use of this call with pupils.

- Invite someone from the emergency services to talk with your pupils.

This story is adapted from an article in the TES, 5 January, 2001, about young people who received a Diana Princess of Wales Memorial Award for outstanding contribution to their school or community. All schools and colleges in the UK with pupils in the 12 – 18 age group can nominate a pupil, or group of pupils, for the award. For more information, contact: Education Extra, telephone 020 8709 9935, email: info@educationextra.org.uk.

John Thelwell (on the right of the picture) doesn't look like a hero, but in August 1999 he saved the life of his friend Lee.

One afternoon, while John, Lee and their friend Jamie were riding their bikes in the park, Lee's bike hit a tree stump. He went over the handlebars of his bike, skidded along the ground and hit a curb. He lost an ear, punctured a lung, had serious head injuries and lay bleeding and dying before his two hysterical friends.

John was horrified, but managed to pull himself together enough to remember what he had been told about life-saving when he'd spent a day with the emergency services in Year 6. He put Lee into the recovery position, put his own jacket over him to keep him warm and told Jamie to go for help. But none of the people passing by took any notice of Jamie – they thought he was having a joke.

John calmed his friend down and told him to keep talking to Lee while he tried to get help. Eventually he managed to persuade two men getting out of a car to phone for an ambulance on their mobile. The hospital staff said that without John's initiative Lee would have died. John continued to care for his friend, visiting him during the seven weeks he was in hospital, encouraging him once he was out. When Lee returned to school John was extremely protective of him.

What would you like to say to John?

Where would you go for help if this happened to you?

Do you know first aid?

Why do you think people took no notice of Jamie?

What would you have done in this situation?

Who are the best people to ask for help?

If you dialled 999, who would you ask for and what would you say?

Objectives: To raise awareness of the age-related laws relevant to their age group. To develop awareness of the law and what it means.

Materials: Copies of **Your legal rights** (page 116).

Introduction

Talk about 'the law'. What do your pupils understand by something being 'against the law'? Explore this with examples, e.g. drunk driving, stealing.

Activity 1

- Read through Your legal rights. Pupils have to match the age with the law.

- In pairs, pupils discuss the laws and decide what age they have the legal right.

Plenary

Pupils share their answers.

Activity 2

- Pairs of pupils can then either:
  - pick one law they didn't know, or
  - pick one law which they think is the most important.
- Then two pairs make a group of four.
- Pupils share the laws they have each identified:
  - as being previously unknown to them, or
  - the laws they think are the most important.
  - They discuss these and how they feel about them.
- Pupils draw or write about one of the laws they have chosen,
- Or they make up a play which shows the law in action.

Plenary

- Pupils share the laws they have chosen as being new to them or of most importance.

- Talk about the implications of these laws for them.

- Are there any things that they wish were law?

- Invite a speaker, e.g. policeman, local magistrate, from the Citizens Advice Bureau, to talk about young people and the law.

- The organisation 'Citizenship Foundation' has many resources on young people and the law (see Resources page 127).

Answers: 1d, 2b, 3g, 4e, 5a, 6f, 7c

Your legal rights

Match the ages to the legal right.

Answer each question about the age at which these rights apply to you, by selecting from the answers, a – g, at the bottom of the page.

1. Every child's birth and name should be registered and a birth certificate issued by the time a child is ....

2. In England, Wales and Northern Ireland, children under .... years are not usually charged with a crime.

If a child's parents or guardians say their child is 'out of control' the child can be brought before a youth court and taken into care.

3. Children at the age of .... can be considered responsible for a crime if there is evidence to show that they knew what they were doing.

4. At the age of .... children can buy a pet animal.

5. Children under .... years should not be working except for odd jobs for family and neighbours.

If children perform in a film or a play, they must have a special licence from their Local Authority.

6. Up to the age of .... children are only allowed in a pub with an adult. The pub must have a children's licence. Children must leave by 9.00 pm.

7. Until a child is .... their parents have to give permission for medical treatment, unless the doctor thinks the child understands what is happening.

a. 13 years old

b. under 9 years old

c. 16 years old

d. 6 weeks old

e. 12 years old

f. 14 years old

g. 10 years old

Running a campaign

In this activity, pupils plan and run a campaign about an issue that they feel strongly about. The teacher will need to decide if the class work together on one campaign or if pupils work in groups on several different campaigns. Cost may be an issue here. This would be a good activity to do at the end of the summer term.

Objective: To help pupils:

- Work together to make their voices heard;
- Plan and run a campaign and be accountable for their actions;
- Evaluate the effectiveness of their campaign and learn for the future.

Materials: Copies of **The Bodozal Project - Brazil** (page 119), copies of **Running a campaign** (pages120-121).

Introduction

Read your pupils the story The Bodozal Project - Brazil, you could also refer to the Children's Peace Movement in Colombia (page 43).

- Discuss the different reason why people run campaigns.
- Thought-shower issues pupils feel strongly about. Write the ideas on a board.
- Discuss each idea and let pupils vote on the one they feel is the most important to them. As a result of the ballot, decide on the issue/s for the campaign.

Activity 1 - Beginning the planning

Before you begin, give the pupils a time plan/schedule for the activity and, if appropriate, suggest they can use non-class time to work on the campaign.

As a class discuss the many ways campaigns can be run, they can have several parts or just one event. Pupils need to think about the main events of the campaign and decide if they will: make posters, make speeches, invite a speaker, ask people's opinion through a questionnaire, produce a leaflet, etc.

Working as a class or in campaign-groups, pupils discuss and decide the following:

- The issue for the campaign.
- What they need to find out about the issue.
- What do they want to achieve?
- Dates for the beginning and end of the campaign.
- Who will be involved in the campaign?
- What will the actions/events of the campaign be?

continued...

- Is a budget needed to run the campaign? What for? How much?
- If so, how will the cost be met?

Activity 2 - Group planning

Using the **Running a campaign** sheets (pages 120-121), pupils plan, prepare and roll out their campaign.

Plenary

Make time for each group to report backs on their progress at regular intervals.

Evaluation of the campaign

It is important to evaluate the campaign's strengths and weaknesses. This sample form might help.

Name of the campaign	What we did	Number of people who attended/ listened/read the poster, etc.	Feedback – what people have said about the campaign	Results of the campaign – did it achieve its aims?
Campaign to improve the playground.	1. We produced a questionnaire. 2. We did an assembly about the campaign. 3. We got everyone to fill in a questionnaire. 4. We analysed the questionnaire. 5. We took the results to the school council and asked if money could be allocated to buy the equipment asked for...	Everyone was really interested, most children (100) answered the questionnaire really well.	Everyone said it was a really good campaign. We could have made the questionnaire a bit easier for everyone to understand.	Yes. We got the new equipment that everyone had helped to choose.

The Bodozal Project – Brazil

Pupils at the Escola Teresinha de Moura, in a poor district of the city of Manaus, Brazil, have made an important improvement to their neighbourhood by cleaning up the Bodozal stream that runs through the heart of it. Everyone who lived beside the stream threw their rubbish, including scraps of food, into it so that it smelled, was very unhealthy and also got blocked so it flooded when rain was heavy.

The young people realised that clearing the stream was one thing, but keeping it clear was another, and they would have to change the behaviour of the people in the neighbourhood. Not everyone understood what the children were trying to do and said, "We don't throw our rubbish in the stream, but our neighbours do."

To explain the importance of keeping the stream clear, the group used different methods with different age groups. With children they used puppets and with adolescents they used dance and drama. They went from house to house to talk to adults. It was difficult because not everyone would listen.

Then, in April 2000, an important event occurred which made the community stop and think. Because of heavy rain there were floods in Manaus, but for the first time the community beside the stream did not flood. People were asking why they didn't get flooded and the children told them it was because the stream wasn't blocked with rubbish so the water could run away. Now the neighbourhood could see the importance of what the children had achieved.

The mayor of Manaus congratulated all the young people involved and asked them to march through the streets of Manaus with banners. Now the pupils are working on educating people about the importance of hygiene and environmental health. Walquiria, aged 12, said,

"Everybody should preserve the natural environment because if we don't we are going to lose our planet."

Running a campaign

Our campaign to ....

You won't need to do everything on this list, just look at the suggestions for the events you are going to do as part of your campaign. Tick the boxes for the actions you decide to take.

1. Do you need to find out more about things to do with your campaign? ☐

What do you need to find out? ....

Who is going to do it? ....

How and where are they going to do it? ....

By when? ....

How will you use the research? ....

2. Do you need posters and badges to make people interested in your campaign, or maybe to get them to a meeting? ☐

Who will do them? ....

Where will you put them or give them out? ....

How many do you need? ....

When do you need them by? ....

3. Will you write letters to important people and the media? ☐

Who will you write letters to? ....

Who will write them? ....

When should they be sent? ....

N.B. If you want a reply to your letter make sure you ask a question that has to be answered.

4. Will you conduct a questionnaire to find out what people think? ☐

What do you want to find out? ....

Who will design it? ....

When will you do it, and to whom? ....

How many questionnaires will you make? ....

How will you analyse it? ....

What will you do with the results? ....

5. Will you hold a big event, e.g. a concert, or a rally with speakers? ☐

What kind of event will you hold? ....

When and where will it be? ....

Who will perform or speak? ....

Who do you want to come? ....

Running a campaign

Organising an event or public meeting

If you want to organise an event or public meeting (this means a meeting that anyone can come to) consider these questions and note down your answers:

What will be the purpose of the meeting?

Who will be your speaker/s at the meeting?

Where and when will the meeting be?

Who will book the room?

Who do you want to come?

How will you get people to the meeting? Will you use posters, leaflets, loud speakers?

Will you send invitations to important people you really want to be there?

Who needs to receive an invitation?

Who will write the invitations?

Decide on a programme for the meeting.

Appoint a leader/chairperson to keep you on-task.

Who will get the room ready and see there are enough chairs, a table, a microphone, water for the speakers?

Will you produce a programme? Who will write it? How will you make enough copies?

Who will welcome guests and show them to their seats?

Who will look after the speaker/s?

Rehearse introductions/speeches, etc.

5.6

Say Yes for children

Objective: For pupils to think about their rights and prioritise three which they would like to bring to the attention of world leaders.

Materials: Copies of **Say Yes for children** (page 123)

Introduction

Say Yes was the global campaign to collect millions of pledges of support for children's rights world-wide in the run up to the UN Special Session for Children in 2002. The aim of the campaign was to demonstrate massive public support for governments to take real action at the UN Special Session and improve the lives of millions of children.

Millions of people around the globe made a pledge and although the Special Session is over, the 10 action points that were used to collect pledges is still as appropriate and your pupils could discuss which of three they would select.

- **Prepare your pupils by reading through each statement first. Some of them may seem a little similar and may need some discussion.**

Activity

Photocopy the Say yes form and give one to groups of your pupils and ask them to discuss and decide which three they would tick.

1. Leave no child out	6. Listen to children
2. Put children first	7. Educate every child
3. Care for every child	8. Protect children from war
4. Fight HIV/AIDS	9. Protect the earth for children
5. Stop harming and exploiting children	10. Fight poverty: invest in children

Plenary

- Pupils share their choices and say why they made them.
- A bar chart could be made ranking the number of elections for each one.

Say Yes for children

Colour in the three most urgent issues for you.

I, ...

believe that all children should be free to grow in health, peace and dignity, and that we must:

1 ——————Leave no child out

2 ——————Put children first

3 ——————Care for every child

4 ——————Fight HIV/AIDS

5 ——————Stop harming and exploiting children

6 ——————Listen to children

7 ——————Educate every child

8 ——————Protect children from war

9 ——————Protect the earth for children

10 ——————Fight poverty: invest in children

Good citizens, global citizens

This section suggests ways children can extend their new knowledge and skills into the community and wider environment and share what they learn.

Research

- Using family links, local connections and the Internet, find out about laws for children in other countries and compare them to our existing laws.

- Design a questionnaire/quiz on "laws for children" and try it on different audiences, e.g. other pupils, parents, passersby. Tabulate the results and do a report.

- Read the poem Human Rights (page 125). This has specific reference to the Human Rights Act which came into force in the UK in October 2000. Pupils could do research into what it says and what the implications are for pupils and teachers and schools. This could be presented to the school, governors and parents.

- Using the work developed round the story of Hidden Hero (page 114), devise a play for assembly that reflects information from this unit about what to do in an emergency.

- Invite a local councillor to visit to answer questions about local facilities for young people then share this with the rest of the school.

- Prepare an end-of-term performance using information and skills gained from doing this work.

Homework

- Pupils give their quiz about young people's legal rights to their family at home.

- Pupils ask their parents what their communities were like when they were young. Did they feel part of the community?

- Pupils ask their parents how they see the community they live in. Do they do anything to contribute? What improvements would they like in their community?

- Pupils share the poem, 'Human Rights', and ask the family to help them write their own poem.

Human Rights

I am not very old
But I think I understand
How the Human Rights Act
Would work throughout the land.

Freedom within the law
To work and think and pray.
To speak out against injustice
Which many suffer from each day.

I am still a child
But I think I know what's right,
Like standing up for friends
When a bully wants to fight.

We must all work together
To create a better place.
So that all people, everywhere
Can have a living space.

Life is very precious.
We all have much to give.
We must care for one another
And must live and let live.

By Alan Barry (aged 11)

Resources and addresses

Save the Children resources

Partners in Rights £15.00 - Creative activities exploring citizenship for 7-11s, drawing on the insights of children in Latin America and the UK, containing photocards, activity sheets and detailed guidance.

Families Pack £15.00 - contains family stories about four children from across the world. There are full colour photo sheets; differentiated activities; a teacher's book and cross-curricular guidelines exploring moral, social, cultural and spiritual issues for children of all abilities.

Young Citizen's Pack £15.00 - features children who have each taken action on an issue that they care about in Honduras, Uganda, Guatemala, India and the UK – the pack contains 16 colour photo cards and a teacher support section designed to bring out global dimensions in citizenship.

Rights and Responsibilities Teacher's Handbook £6.00 - As citizenship becomes an integral part of primary education, this handbook will prove a key resource in every primary classroom. What are rights and how are they related to responsibilities? Find out through a range of stories, facts and activities.

The School Council – a Children's Guide £5.00 - explains how to create your own school council, it has case studies, ideas for elections and details of the UN Convention on the Rights of the Child, and features children's words and artwork.

Save the Children's Eye to Eye website
www.savethechildren.org.uk/eyetoeye features photographs and stories told by young Palestinian refugees and a teacher's section which has background information on the Palestinian – Israeli conflict, guidance on dealing with sensitive issues and lesson plans aimed specifically at citizenship for Key Stages 2 and 3.

Taking Action: Save the Children £9.99 - behind the scenes of how the organisation works; published with Heinemann. Primary reader.

Speaking Out is Save the Children's free volunteer speaker service for citizenship and global development issues. To enquire about a speaker contact the Schools Administrator on 0207 703 5400 x2588

For advice on curriculum issues call the Education Unit on 0207 703 5400 ext 2867. email education@scfuk.org.uk

To order Save the Children's education catalogues and publications contact:
Plymbridge Distribution Ltd
Estover Road
Plymouth PL6 7PY
Tel: 01752 202 301
Fax: 01752 202 333
Email: orders@plymbridge.com

UNICEF resources

What Rights?
Summary of the Convention on the Rights of the Child for young people. Order code 32021. Free

Wants and needs cards
Ten sets of 20 cards in five different colours. Cards are ready made copies of those used in the activity in Unit 1. The cards come with an instruction sheet and summary of the Convention on the Rights of the Child, packed in a resealable plastic wallet. Order code 35161. £8.00

India: Children's needs; children's rights
This pan-India, cross-curricular resource is designed around the lives of six *partner* children in India from widely varying backgrounds and locations. A rights perspective is brought to units looking at habitat and standard of living, water and health, who can afford a healthy diet, going to school in India, and play time. Also children's festivals, mendhi and world faiths.
- 110 page Teacher's Book with photocopiable pupils sheets;
- 15 A4 colour photo sheets with activities and information on the reverse;
- *A Journey through India* full-colour educational board game;

- Activities at three levels: 5-8 yrs, 9-11 yrs, 12-14 yrs relating to: geography/people and place, people in society/citizenship, English, maths, science, RE, healthy and safe living, art/design & technology. Order code 35157. £10.00

It's Only Right: This book published by UNICEF's international Education for Development Unit, provides a practical guide for learning about the UN Convention on the Rights of the Child and using it as a springboard for action. Contains 15 activities. Order code 36083. £5.00

Raised Voices - video
Under the UN Convention on the Rights of the Child every child has a right to express an opinion. This video contains four self-contained films of how children are taking up this right: in South Africa children create a children's charter which was incorporated into South Africa's Constitution; in the USA a high school student talks to her peers about the need for accurate information after contracting HIV from her haemophiliac boyfriend; primary school children in Liverpool take control of their local environmental problems; street children in Brazil take their concerns to the National Assembly.
Order code 17013. 30 minutes, £6.50

Resources and addresses

What is UNICEF? - video
A lively video for primary age children designed to explain the work of UNICEF, including the UN Convention on the Rights of the Child. Children talk to actor, Vas Blackwood, about filtering water, a nutritious diet, and healthcare, supported by film footage from Nigeria, Bangladesh, Colombia and Angola and archive footage to look at the origins of UNICEF in 1946. Order code 37011. 27 minutes, £6.50

The Meena Videos
A number of these cartoon videos are available from UNICEF on request, £6.00 each

Thursday's Child
Thursday's Child is both a full musical and a choral work for young people on the theme of children's rights. The story follows a group of children who make a journey to happiness, on the way encountering situations which illustrate the worst aspects of life for child around the world; children love it!
Teachers' Pack: video of a performance with stopping points for discussion, Teachers' Book (48 pages) and a poster. Order code 35029. Price £17.50.
Performance Pack: everything you need to put on a performance: score, script, backing CD and poster. Order code 35019. Price £45.00
Performance CD: songs from the musical. Order code 38019. Price £13.00
Songbook: piano version of selected songs, with narration for a cantata performance. Free CD with backing track and a sung performance. Order code 36049. Price £16.00

World Map
Peters Projection world map, 84cm x 60cm. Order code 31066 £4.00

Global Topics for literacy hour
12 x A2 big colour photos depicting aspects of life in Colombia, Indonesia and Tanzania of interest to children. On the reverse of each photo are 4 x A4 photocopiable pages, each one the basis for one week's work in literacy hour. The reverse of each photo consists of :
- High Frequency word list for Reception, Years 1 & 2, Years 4 & 5;
- A wide range of activities to support Word and Text level work.
PLUS three topic books for cross-curricular work with photocopiable activity sheets and a Teacher's Guide linking Literacy Hour material, the big photographs and topic work. Order code. 35939 £5.00

Songs, games and stories from around the world
An audio cassette of 17 songs sung in many languages with a book containing the lyrics and music nototation, 15 games and 13 stories. Order code 38010. £6.50

To order UNICEF catalogues and resources, contact:
Unit 1 Rignals Lane,
Chelmsford,
CM2 8TU
Tel: 0870 606 3377 Fax: 01245 477394
Order online on www.unicef.org.uk

To find out about UNICEF's free service for classroom sessions or inservice training about children's rights and global development issues, call 0207 405 5592. email education@unicef.org.uk

Other useful addresses

Childline
2nd Floor
Royal Mail Building
Studd Street
London N1 OQW
Tel: 0207 239 1001

Citizenship Foundation
Ferroners House
Shaftesbury Place
London EC2Y 8AA
Tel: 0207 367 0500

LEAP Confronting Conflict Project
The Lab
8 Lennox Road
London N4 3NW
Tel: 0207 272 5630

Mediation UK
Alexander House
Telephone Avenue
Bristol BS1 4BS
Tel: 0117 904 6661

(Mediation UK have a directory of conflict resolution/mediation service providers.)

National Children's Bureau
8 Wakely Street
London EC1V 7QE
Tel: 0207 278 9512
(Article 12 is also at this address)

NSPCC
42 Curtain Road
London EC2A 3NH
Tel: 0207 825 2500

Schools Councils UK
57 Etchingham Park Road
London N3 2EB
Tel: 0208 349 2459
Fax: 0208 346 0898